INTERVALLIC FRETBOARD

Towards improvising on the Guitar

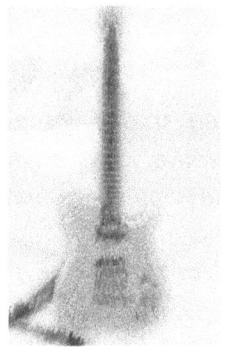

Ashkan Mashhour

Dave H. Murdy

Copyright © 2007, 2010 by Ashkan Mashhour and Dave H. Murdy

•••••••

"I wish I would have had this book as a kid during my quest for the understanding of improvising and being able to fluidly solo through all the chord changes with ease. This book can open some new doors for those guitarists who have hit a 'brick wall' in that quest."
–BRENT MASON, Studio & Solo guitarist

"This book shows all the important aspects and structures necessary to get into improvising on the instrument. I strongly recommend it to everyone interested in starting and developing their skills towards expressing themselves on the guitar."
–BIRÉLI LAGRÈNE, Jazz/Gypsy Jazz guitarist

"Dave and Ashkan have done an amazing job putting an essential subject for any improvising musician into a clearly understandable form. I highly recommend it for anyone serious about self-expression through music."
–BRETT GARSED, Rock/Fusion guitarist

*"*Intervallic Fretboard *offers the aspiring student of jazz and rock guitar improvisation an enlightened approach to generating creative ideas on their instrument and learning to think outside the typical guitar 'box'. An outstanding resource for the guitar's unique geometric symmetry and the critical training of the mind's ear."*
–JIMMY BROWN, Senior Editor, Guitar World magazine

"I just finished Intervallic Fretboard*, and now can't wait to talk about it and share some of the concepts with my 'Functional Skills for Studio Guitarists Class'. The chapter on 'anchors', and the Rhythm Ology étude are worth the price of the book alone. A fresh approach to some of the trickier concepts of our instrument – I highly recommend it to mature, or maturing guitarists."*
–RICHARD SMITH, Professor of Studio/Jazz guitar, University of Southern California

•••••••

INTERVALLIC FRETBOARD

Towards improvising on the Guitar

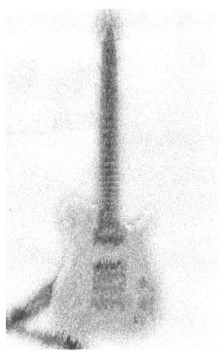

Ashkan Mashhour
Dave H. Murdy

Inquiries: **ashkan@cheatsheetmusic.com**

Cover & interior design, typography,
illustration, photography, music engraving, prepress:
Ashkan Mashhour

CD recording: Ashkan Mashhour & Dave Murdy
CD mixing, mastering: Ashkan Mashhour
Ashkan Mashhour (guitar), Dave Murdy (guitar, bass), Dan Murdy (drums)
CD/audio available separately

www.intervallicfretboard.com

ISBN: 978-0-9830498-0-7

First edition

Copyright © 2007, 2010 Ashkan Mashhour and Dave H. Murdy. Published by Pêle-Mêle Works.
All rights reserved. No part of this book may be reproduced or distributed in any form or by any means, or stored in a database or retrieval system, without prior written consent of the authors, including, but not limited to, in any network or other electronic storage or transmission, or broadcast for distance learning.

About the authors

Ashkan Mashhour received his "Diplôme d'Ingénieur" from ENST Bretagne, France and his MSc from University College London, U.K., both in 1997. He has since held R&D and programme management positions in the field of RF and digital communications in the wireless and semiconductor industries.

Ashkan has been an avid student of the guitar since his late teens. He has taken numerous courses in music and performance, both in private and ensemble settings, including at Orange Coast College in Costa Mesa, California. He has also developed the CHEATSHEET Music™ series of music instructional products.

Dave Murdy received his BM in jazz and commercial guitar from the University of Southern California, in 1984. Since graduating, Dave has gone on to lead a very diverse musical career.

Dave was an original member of Kilauea, a very successful pop jazz outfit he toured the country with and performed on four CDs, two of which went top 10 on the Billboard charts. While with Kilauea, Dave released his own jazz CD: "That Goes To Show Ya". He later released two CDs with his trio Toxic Jazz and currently performs with The Big Band Wartime Radio and Tijuana Dogs, a very popular Orange County based pop and rock band.

Dave has performed and recorded with a wide range of artists from jazz, classical, to pop, rock and country music. Artists include Art Davis, Brandon Fields, Eric Marienthal, Tony Guerrero, Bobby Shew, Warren Hill, as well as 60s pop stars Mel Carter and Jackie Deshannon, Steely and others.

Dave is very active as a session musician, playing on numerous independent releases, and as an arranger and writer. He has written, arranged, and recorded original music for Universal Studios theme parks, and composed soundtrack for "Muzak", heard around the world.

Throughout his career, Dave has been committed to education as a guitar instructor and clinician and presently teaches as an Adjunct Faculty member at Orange Coast College and to a wide array of private students.

Acknowledgements

Writing a book is an intimidating project, so much so that it often fails to materialise or even begin, if not for a triggering agent. For me, this catalyst was my guitar teacher, Dave Murdy. I first encountered Dave at his Studio Guitar class at Orange Coast College and his vast musical knowledge and experience, not to mention his fine guitar playing and open-mindedness never stopped short of inspiring me. Thanks Dave.

In Southern California, I also learnt a great deal from Mark Wein and Jay Simper, at their Rhythm & Groove class – it really is fun to play with a band! John Schneiderman at Orange Coast College broadened my musical tastes through his ensemble class. I also wish to thank my "musical buddies" over the last few years, namely John Pollard, Cain German, Ryan Kossler, Mike Nasr, Daniel Ferris, and James Friedman.
But for me, the journey started many years earlier, in France, when I tiptoed on the guitar with my friend Thierry Chebat and later got my first memorable lessons with Ludovic Mesnil and Jean-Pierre Mallet, which, unbeknownst to them, only incited me to learn and practise more.

I was mesmerised when guitar greats Brent Mason, Brett Garsed, and Biréli Lagrène, as well as Jimmy Brown of Guitar World and Prof. Richard Smith of USC accepted to review the book. I can't thank you enough...because I still can't believe it!
Special thanks to Markus Weiss for help coordinating the review with Biréli behind the scenes.

Last, but foremost, my heartfelt thanks are for my parents, Azy and Vahid, who have always supported me in whatever venture I set my mind on. Merci du fond du cœur!

Los Angeles, May 2010
Ashkan Mashhour.

••••••••

I would like to thank my late teacher and mentor Reed Gilchrist for widening my understanding of the instrument and instilling a real love for the Guitar in me.
I would like to thank my parents Bob and Kay Murdy for always supporting me in my endeavors.
I would like to thank my wife Jackie Murdy for always encouraging me to go after my dreams.
Special thanks to John Picetti at Dean Markley.
Special thanks to C.B. Hill at C.B. Hill Guitars.
Thanks to Dan Murdy for the Drum tracks on "Intervallick Rock" and "Rhythm Ology" on the accompanying CD. Drums recorded at Back Alley Studios, Whittier, California.
A special thanks to my long time dear friend and virtuoso classical guitarist Scott Tennant for his endorsement and suggestions.
To all my colleagues at Orange Coast College, especially the late John McEnary as well as Joe Poshek and Dana Wheaton.
Thank you!!

Los Angeles, May 2010
Dave H. Murdy.

Table of contents

About the authors 4
Acknowledgements 5
Table of contents 6
Foreword 7
The sweet beginning 8

1 On intervals: some definitions and terminology 9
    Interval 9
    Simple and compound intervals 12
    Inversion 14

2 String intervals 17
    Shortcomings of patterns and shapes 17
    Adjacent string intervals 18
    The 3rd–2nd string "paradigm" shift 18
    Developing intervallic fluency 19
    Stacking intervals: triads...and beyond 29

3 Chords revisited: exploiting tonal distance 35
    Chord tone and scale tone movement of chords – triads and 7th chords 35
    Further chordal insight 43
    Visualising chords: chord tones 45

4 Interval-based scale and chord derivation: the anchoring principle 47
    Scale derivation 47
    Chord/arpeggio derivation 58
    When the single line meets the harmony: chord-melody 61

5 "Lessons learnt!" 63
    Points to remember 63
    The "intervallic fluency test" 64

6 Chord-melody étude 66

7 Intervallick Rock 69
    Chord progression 70
    Melody line 70

8 "Rhythm Ology" 75
    Why this song? 75
    Brief song analysis 75
    Piecing it all together: applying jazz improvisation techniques through an intervallic thought process – commented solo 78
    Chord comping over "Rhythm Ology" 88

APPENDICES
    A   Interval jogger 93
    B   Interval-based notation system 94
          Position playing 94
          Description of the system 97
    C   Common and less common scales & modes 100
    D   Common chord formulae & symbols 101

Notation guide 102

References and further reading 103

The end (not bitter!)... 104

Foreword

It is sometimes said about the guitar as being amongst the easiest instruments to learn, yet one of the hardest to master. Such a statement certainly more than hints at the truth in many ways.

To benefit from this book, the reader must be somewhat familiar with music theory and harmony, in particular scale and chord construction, the guitar fretboard and note location, have tinkered with improvisation, and demonstrate enough technical ability on the guitar.

The book is organised around an initial improvisation situation, from which stems an exploratory path founded on intervals, designed to tackle that very situation. This path exposes the strong coupling that exists between the knowledge of intervals and their applicability to the guitar fingerboard. The book concludes by returning to the opening improvisation challenge and applying the intervallic concepts developed throughout.

Chapters incrementally building on one another, it is recommended to go through them in sequence. However, early acquaintance with the interval-based notation system described in Appendix B will serve you throughout the book.

A particular effort was made to present the material in a concise manner, illustrating it with limited but meaningful examples in order to let the concepts stand out, uncluttered. Thus encouraging the student to expand on and experiment. Likewise, ornamentation was left out for the most part, letting the focus be on the notes in hand.

The fruit of the interaction of a student with his teacher, this book attempts to close the knowledge gap by breaking down the concepts into piecemeal steps, answering many questions and needs a student may have with respect to the material being covered. Hopefully, this will offer an effective pedagogical balance.

Everyone learns at their own pace, has more or less facility in certain areas, and all will encounter months of apparent stagnation and frustration. Music is a lifelong journey, for the student, the teacher...and the audience. We are all learning. Savour every moment of it and persevere – you won't regret it!

*An accompanying **CD/audio** is available for all music examples. Please consult the website: www.intervallicfretboard.com*

The sweet beginning

One day, while taking private lessons, my teacher who happened to be no other than Dave Murdy, gave me the lead sheet for Anthropology, a jazz standard by Charlie Parker and Dizzy Gillespie. The assignment was: "Improvise in the 5th position, emphasising guide tones (3rds and 7ths of each chord) and attempt to lean smoothly into the next chord by a whole or a half step, ending and beginning each chord on a guide tone". The piece was in the key of B♭ major except for the bridge, which was "modulating" with a succession of two-bar dominant chords in fourths.

For me, this was a tough challenge: I understood exactly what I was to do but needed so much thinking to do before I could play a single note on each chord change that by the time I had the slightest idea, the progression had moved on to the next chord, even at ridiculously slow tempos (nowhere near the Fast Bebop meter of the tune!).

Seeing me agonise, Dave broke down the assignment into smaller, more manageable steps. First, he asked me to only play the guide tones on each chord, then, he asked me to write the B♭ major scale pattern in the 5th position and map out the guide tones for each chord (some of which were outside the key) and pick my notes in this lot. Last, he asked me to work out a solo based on the initial assignment and write it down, ahead of time.

Divide, we did. Conquer, I did not!

I can't say I was successful at the exercise, but it got me thinking. I could see Dave fly through the changes with the most tasteful lines. "How on earth do you do it?", I wondered.

I knew the major scale patterns (or modes) across the fingerboard in five positions starting on the 6th string, but had trouble playing in-between positions and starting on any note of the scale. I knew the chords in the tune but was struggling to find a given chord tone or arpeggio in time. Although I had learnt the fingerboard, I could not associate note names to particular chord tones fast enough.

So I started experimenting...with intervals. After all, everything is built by stacking up intervals.

In the past, I had memorised intervals between adjacent strings, going up or down the strings. I set out to take this further and build on (and up!) this knowledge in order to derive instantly any scale, any chord, in a given position, freeing me from note names, patterns, shapes and the mental gymnastics shifting from one abstraction to another. This is the premise of this book.

1 On intervals: some definitions and terminology

Intervals are omnipresent in this book, and are a vast topic by themselves, which is covered at length in music theory and harmony textbooks. Therefore, the academic definition of intervals is outside the scope of this book. However, on the guitar in particular, some of those definitions and terminology are loosely applied; or applied in ways that do not strictly follow general conventions.
We felt it necessary to highlight those differences, justify why they make sense, and explain some of the terminology specific to this book.

Interval

An *interval* or tonal distance is defined as the difference in pitch between two notes.

When the notes of an interval are played successively, the interval is called **melodic**. In this case, if the lower pitch is played first, followed by the higher pitch, the interval is called an *ascending melodic* interval. If the higher pitch is played first, then the lower pitch, the interval is called a *descending melodic* interval.
When both notes are played simultaneously, the interval is called **harmonic** and sometimes a *double-stop*. See Figure 1.

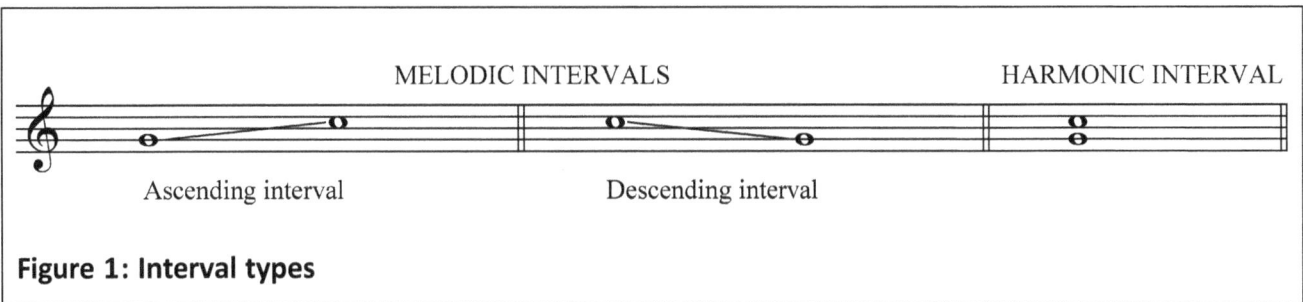

Figure 1: Interval types

The interval is measured by the number of scale tones it contains, which determines the interval **quantity** (e.g. a second, a fourth, a seventh) – this number includes the first and last note in the interval. The number of scale tones contained within an interval is the same whether measured from the lower or upper note of the interval.

The quantity of an interval is a coarse measure; the **quality** of the interval further and fully qualifies the interval. If the upper pitch note belongs to the major scale of the lower pitch note, then the quality of the interval is *perfect* or *major*. If the upper note does not belong to the major scale of the lower note, then the interval is either *minor*, *augmented*, or *diminished* (same applies for both ascending and descending intervals).

1- On intervals: some definitions and terminology

Figure 2 shows various intervals. Note the key signature of G major in Figure 2, since the lower note of the interval is G, that is, except for the last measure, where it is E♭. The last measure is explained in Figure 3: since the lower note is E♭, the interval should be analysed in the key of E♭, although it is written in the key of G. The interval is first shown in the key of G major, where the accidental is required on that note (E♭), but it is not to be mistaken for an adjustment. The same interval is then shown in the second measure in the key of the lower note (E♭); both the lower and upper notes are diatonic to this key. The interval being a 3rd, it is therefore a major 3rd. Table 1 illustrates frequently used interval quantity/quality.

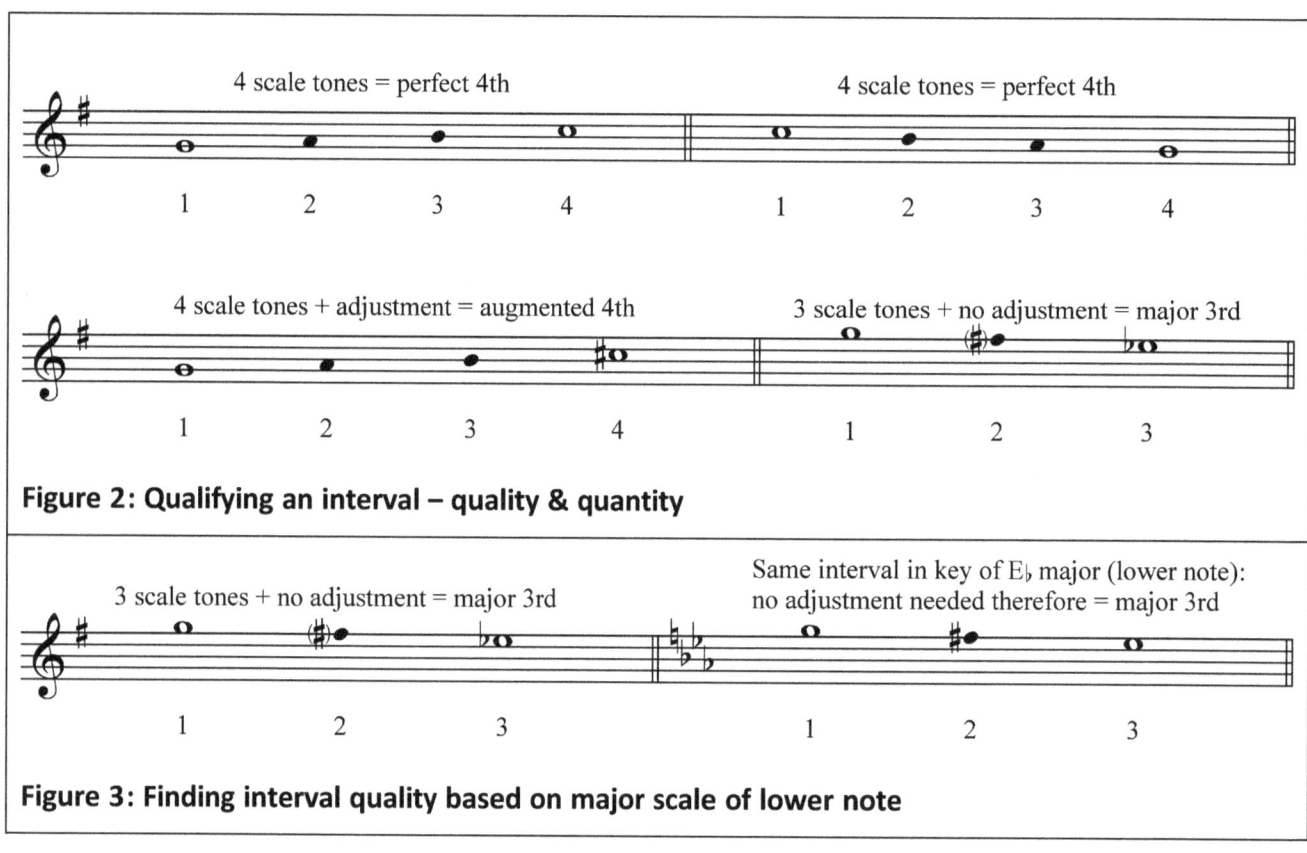

Figure 2: Qualifying an interval – quality & quantity

Figure 3: Finding interval quality based on major scale of lower note

1- On intervals: some definitions and terminology

Number of semitones	Interval quality & quantity
0	unison
1	minor second
2	major second
3	minor third
4	major third
5	perfect fourth
6	augmented fourth (or diminished fifth)
7	perfect fifth
8	minor sixth
9	major sixth
10	minor seventh
11	major seventh
12	octave

Table 1: Interval quality & quantity

Table 1 is only a guideline; intervals can be further modified. For example, a perfect fourth can be lowered enharmonically and will then be named a diminished fourth (same as major third), and some intervals can be lowered by a full step – see Table 2. The interval therefore gets its name from its quantity and its quality. Except for the interval quantities/qualities of Table 1, the usage of most remaining terms in Table 2 is less frequent (e.g. augmented seventh is hardly ever used).

Referenced to lower note's major scale	-1 tone	-½ tone	+0 tone	+½ tone
second		minor	major	augmented
third	diminished	minor	major	augmented
fourth		diminished	perfect	augmented
fifth		diminished	perfect	augmented
sixth	diminished	minor	major	augmented
seventh	diminished	minor	major	augmented
octave		diminished	perfect	augmented

Table 2: Types of interval quality

Intervallic Fretboard – Towards improvising on the Guitar

Simple and compound intervals

Any interval smaller than an octave is a ***simple interval***. An interval extending beyond an octave's range is a ***compound interval***. Every octave added to the simple interval adds the number 7 to the interval quantity (e.g. the compound of a 4th and an octave is a 11th: 4+7=11). Figure 4 shows a simple interval and two compounds built on it. Likewise, the simple interval embedded in a compound interval can be found by subtracting the number 7 from the compound, as many times as necessary for the difference to be smaller than the number 8.

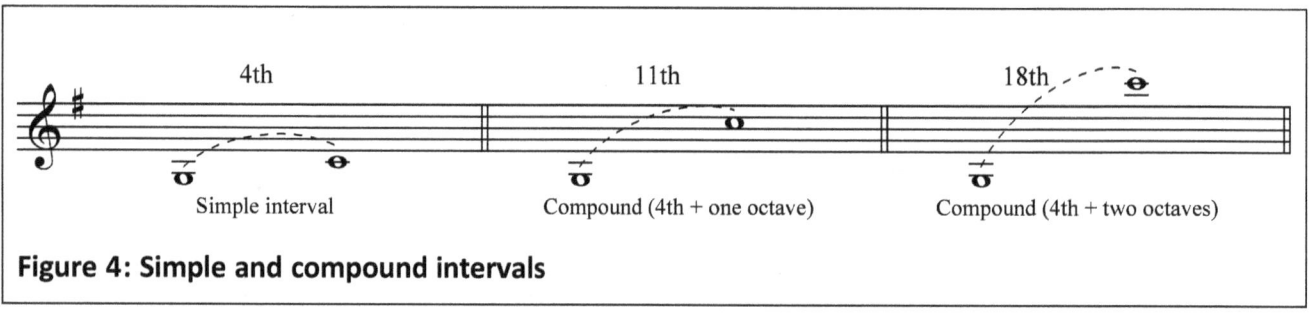

Figure 4: Simple and compound intervals

An important practical difference arises here when it comes to the guitar, especially in music genres such as jazz. When one plays a scale, compound intervals are never referred to: for instance, we say we play the 4th of the G major scale (note C), but we never refer to this note as a 11th or a 18th, even if it is respectively an octave and a perfect fourth or two octaves and a perfect fourth away from the G note used as a reference! (there are a handful of exceptions, which we will mention shortly)

In chords however, compound intervals do find a usage. For example, if the chord made of the tones G-B-D-F-E is played (not necessarily in this order), it is usually called G13 because it contains 1–3–5–♭7–13 degrees of the G major scale. The 13th degree, as voiced in the chord, may not always be an octave and a major sixth away from the G note (root), it could even be in the bass of the chord (inversion)! It would be tempting to call the 13th the 6th degree instead, arguably so. It is simply not done, it is a matter of usage and terminology. Two G13 voicings are given in Figure 5, with the correct notation as well as some tempting incorrect notations using compound intervals pointed out. Note that both voicings omit the 5th.

In fact, if you would go as far as calling this chord G6 instead of G13, it would be plain wrong. G6 is made of the following chord tones: 1–3–5–6, it does not contain the 7th.

1- On intervals: some definitions and terminology

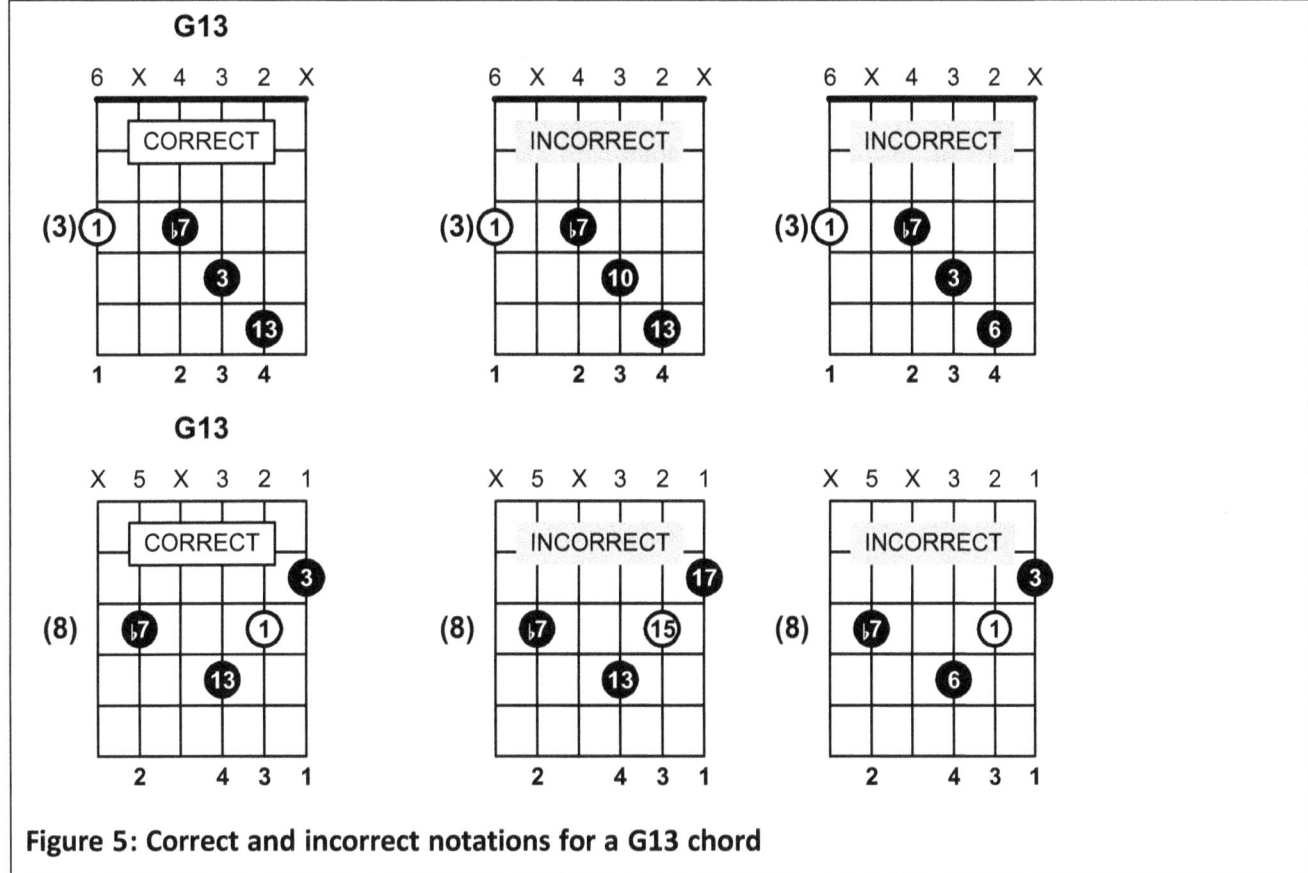

Figure 5: Correct and incorrect notations for a G13 chord

We claimed that compounds are never used when one plays a scale or melody, before alluding to some exceptions. One exception is when one plays a line against a chord, say a G13 chord, and reaches for the note E for example (13th of the chord). In that case, we may refer to playing the 13th, which is no other than the 6th degree of the G major scale. Another exception is when in a melody, we use the term interval as the measure of tonal distance (the distance in pitch between two notes) – for example, if there is a jump of a minor 10th in a melody line, then we say there is an ascending or descending minor 10th in the melody. The interval is indeed a minor 10th (♭10th), not a minor 3rd. Another area where compounds are used in melodies is transposition.

In this book, for the purpose of interval calculations, only simple intervals are used. What matters in those calculations is the harmonic function of the note, which the simple interval does capture. The "IVL" notation (see Appendix B) also only uses simple intervals (you will not see a 9th but a 2nd on the "IVL" staff). In chord notations however, compound intervals are used in the book, as it is a widespread practise to do so.

Inversion

An interval can be **inverted**, by either raising the lowest pitch an octave, or lowering the highest pitch an octave. The sum of an interval and its inversion always amounts to the number 9 (e.g. a major 6th + its inversion a minor 3rd equals 9). In certain ways, an interval and its inversion are complements of one another, adding up to form an octave. See Figure 6.

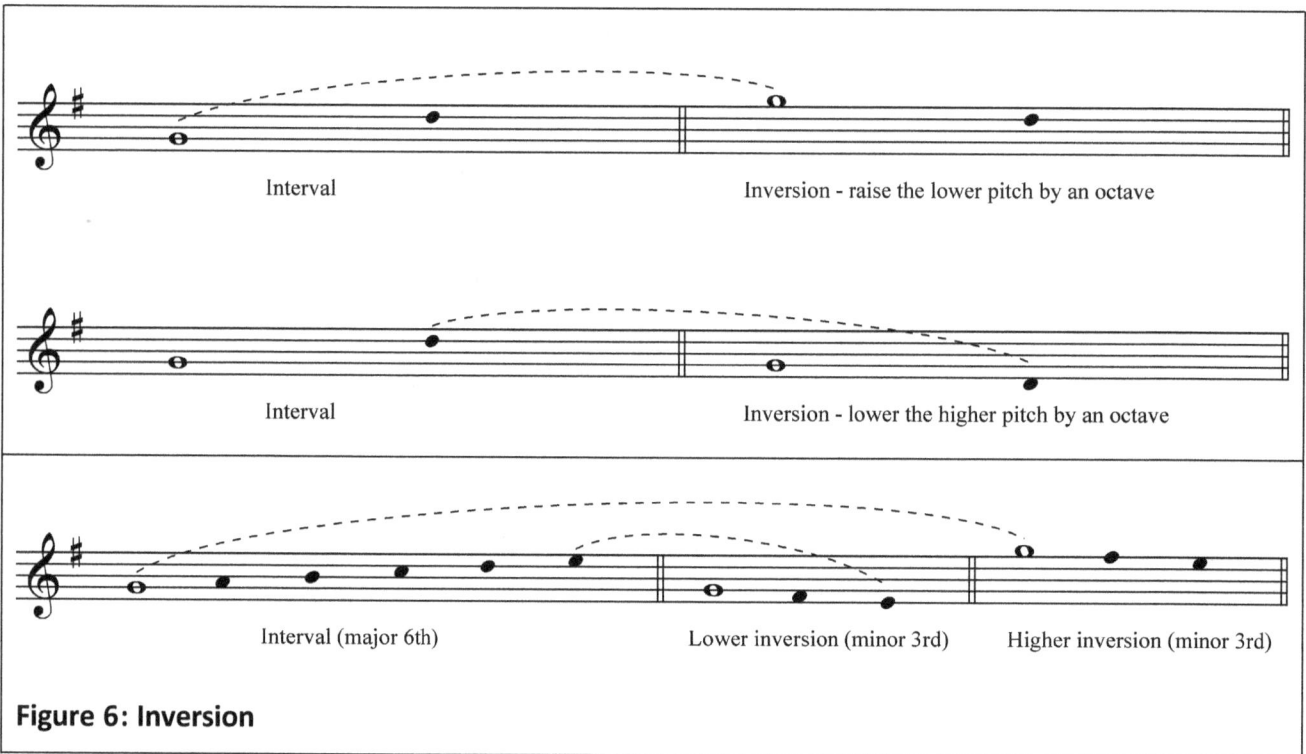

Figure 6: Inversion

Simply remember the following basic rules when inverting an interval:
- Major becomes minor
- Minor becomes major
- Perfect remains perfect
- Augmented becomes diminished and vice versa (or a tritone remains a tritone)

For example, major 3rd becomes minor 6th, minor 2nd becomes major 7th, diminished 5th (same as augmented 4th) becomes augmented 4th etc.

It is important to notice the distinction between ascending/descending interval and an inversion. As can be seen in Figure 7, none of the two possible inversions of the original (ascending) interval correspond to the descending interval. In other words, ascending/descending intervals are not to be confused with an interval and its inversion.

1- On intervals: some definitions and terminology

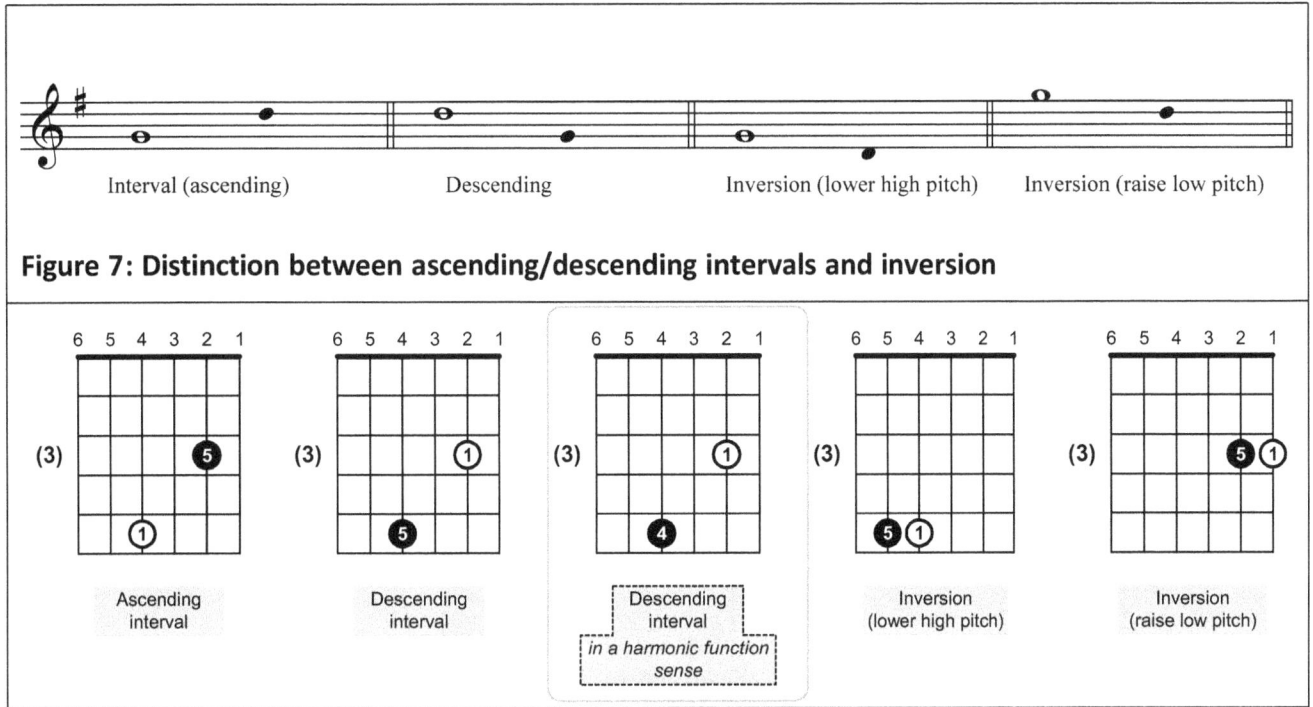

Figure 7: Distinction between ascending/descending intervals and inversion

As we stated earlier, an interval retains the same name (quantity and quality) whether it is ascending or descending. In this book, for the purpose of interval calculation, we will assimilate the ascending interval and its descending counterpart to an interval and its inversion (lower the high pitch) and vice versa. It really isn't an inversion because there is no lowering or raising any of the two pitches by an octave. But there is a valid reason for doing this, and again, its foundation is the harmonic function of the notes at hand and practical terminology used in a playing situation.

For example, in a chord such as the G major triad shown in Figure 8, the chord tones on the 1st, 2nd, and 3rd strings are respectively 1, 5, and 3, in the convention we choose. If the strict definition of an interval was applied, those chord tones, obviously forming descending intervals with the root G (on the 1st string), should be a perfect 4th and a minor 6th away, respectively, from G. This is an interpretation that may stick to the definition, but poorly conveys the harmonic role of the notes. Similarly, if playing a G major scale, the note D would be the 5th of the scale in our convention, regardless of its tonal distance (higher or lower pitch) with respect to the fundamental G. In a sense, there is implicit assimilation of the scale degree with the simple interval formed between the fundamental and that scale degree. What really allows this kind of simplification is the fact that we do away with the compound intervals, because they do not affect the harmonic function of a note.

If we were to use the ascending/descending interval equivalence and compound intervals in describing a scale (mode of G Lydian, with G on 4th string 5th fret as the reference note, i.e. intervals are referred back to that note), we could come up with the notation depicted in Figure 9. It is very clear that the first notation foregoing these two rules – or more accurately, adapting those two rules – is both more practical and more elegant.

1- On intervals: some definitions and terminology

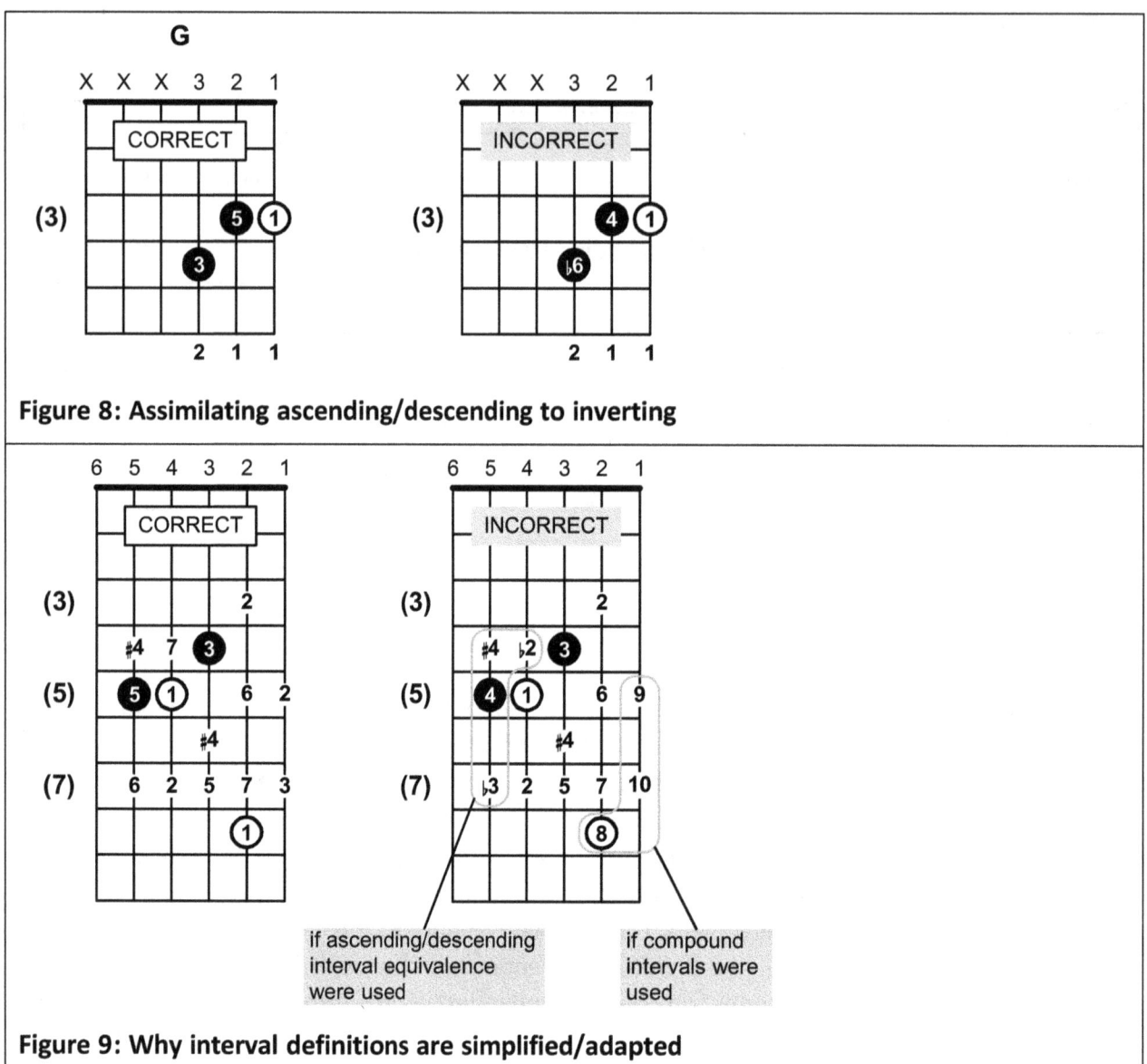

Figure 8: Assimilating ascending/descending to inverting

Figure 9: Why interval definitions are simplified/adapted

As seen from the examples, the terms interval or tonal distance (major 6th), scale degree (6th degree of G major), and chord tone (13th in G13) are often used interchangeably in the musical jargon, which can be misleading. Nevertheless, it is important to distinguish the nuances that set them apart and understand the situations where a lax interpretation of the rules is commonplace.

2 String intervals

Intervals may not jump out at us on a music staff; on the neck of a guitar however, one can take advantage of the rather "visual" or geometric properties of the instrument and bring this essential building block – the interval – to the foreground. Starting with adjacent strings…

Shortcomings of patterns and shapes

Some people have photographic memory, some have auditory memory, and most of us are mildly blessed with either (or neither, really!). The inherent visual nature of the guitar lends itself well to learning patterns for scales or arpeggios and shapes for chords; those are widely taught and do provide some relief as to not having to learn everything in twelve different keys. However, such things as connecting patterns, playing in-between memorised fingerings, starting a pattern on different strings or notes of a scale, knowing the role of each note…and the list goes on, are not only daunting but a real challenge. Apply those to the major scale only and the combinations become endless, let alone learn other scales/modes. Relying solely on shapes is akin speaking a language and not comprehending the words.

Intervals can pave the way to deciphering this limiting visual standpoint. Furthermore, whether you are playing C melodic minor or G♭ melodic minor, the notes making up the scale are different but the formula, in terms of intervals, is just the same; whether you are to play a B13 or a D13, the chord tones are different but once again, the intervallic formula is the same…so why not steer our thinking increasingly towards intervals? The study of intervals leads to more simplicity and logic – it is not a shortcut, au contraire!

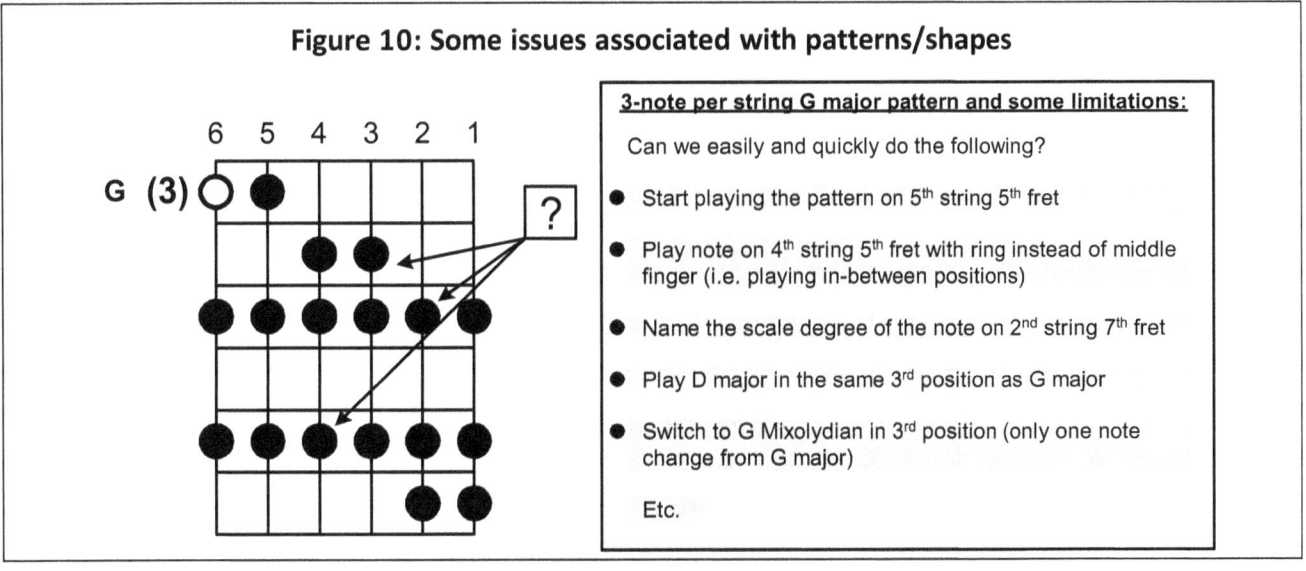

Figure 10: Some issues associated with patterns/shapes

Adjacent string intervals

The guitar's standard tuning (E A D G B E) yields a specific tonal distance or interval between each string. Let us delve into this arrangement.

As shown in Figure 11, an ascending[1] pattern of perfect 4ths is the rule between adjacent strings, except for the 3rd to 2nd string, which is only a major 3rd (half a step or one fret less). Figure 12 shows an identical pattern, descending adjacent strings, in perfect 5ths (5th+4th=octave), except, once again, for the 2nd to the 3rd string, characterised by a minor 6th. **Refer to Chapter 1 for an explanation (section titled "Inversion").**

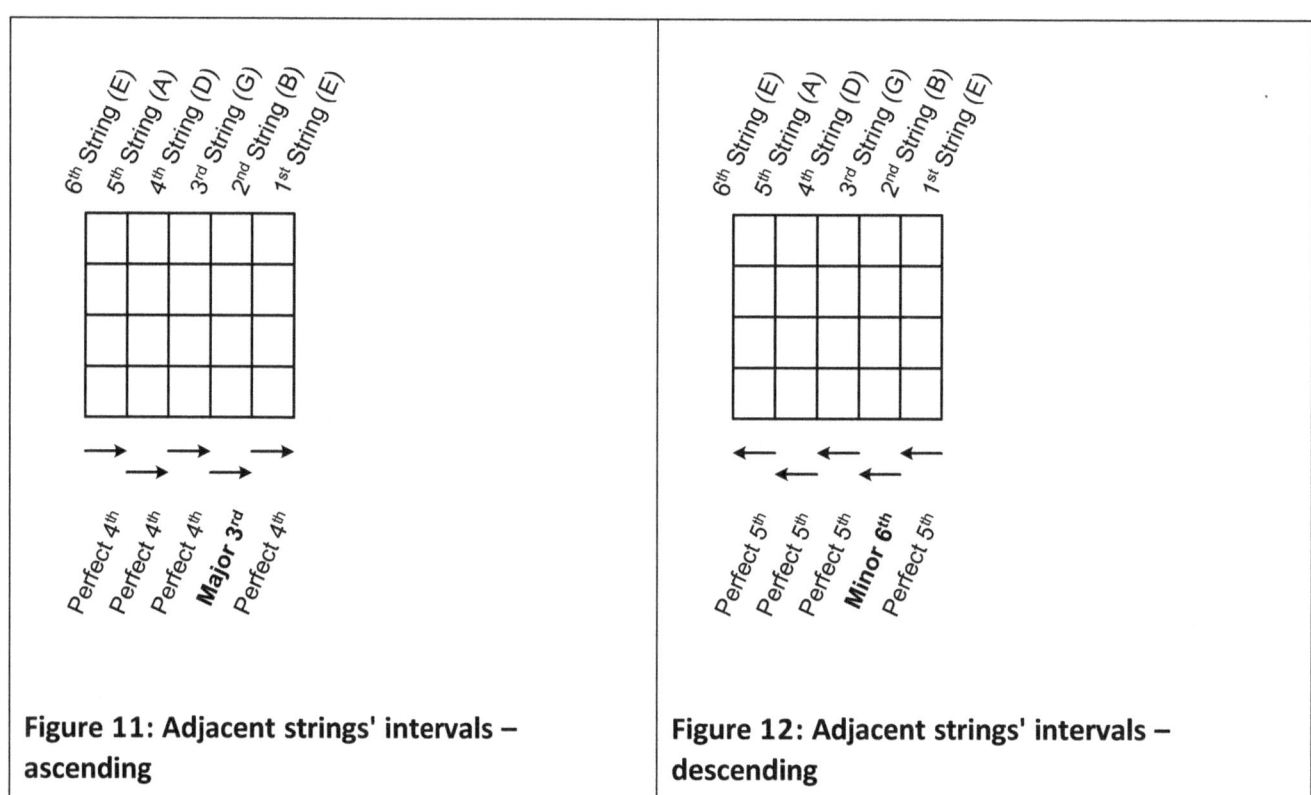

Figure 11: Adjacent strings' intervals – ascending

Figure 12: Adjacent strings' intervals – descending

It is important to commit these intervals to memory, as they are instrumental to the remainder of this book.

The 3rd–2nd string "paradigm" shift

As noted in the opening paragraphs, the interval separating the 3rd and 2nd strings is different from all other adjacent strings: instead of a perfect 4th, it is only a major 3rd (if going from the 2nd to the 3rd string, it is then a minor 6th instead of a perfect 5th) – see Figure 13. This apparently benign shift creates a discontinuity throwing us off in the pursuit of geometrical symmetry of the neck.

---

[1] "ascending" or "up" refer in the text, unless otherwise stated, to moving vertically from low to high pitch strings on the neck; "descending" or "down" would refer to the opposite manoeuvre. A customary convention that defies gravity!

2- String intervals

With a little awareness and practise, we can incorporate this discrepancy into our knowledge of the fretboard (Figure 14).

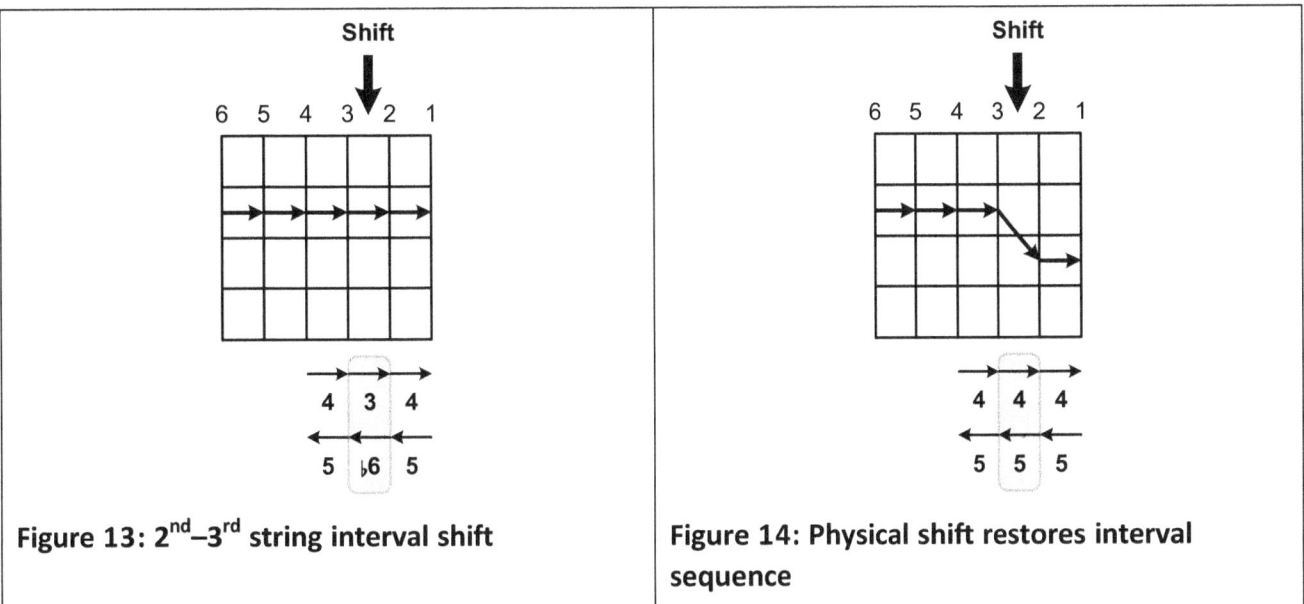

Figure 13: 2nd–3rd string interval shift

Figure 14: Physical shift restores interval sequence

Developing intervallic fluency

<u>Mirroring:</u>
Practise instantly recognising intervals beyond adjacent strings: intervals between strings 2 to 4, strings 4 to 1 etc. As you start skipping more and more strings, the interval between far apart strings will appear harder to process or visualise. A simple trick is to take advantage of the axis of symmetry or "mirror" that is formed by the low and high E string pair. Since a simple and compound interval hold the same harmonic function[2] (e.g. a 4th is viewed as the same as a 11th), the low and high E strings of the guitar are virtually the same string, for the purpose of identifying intervals. This greatly simplifies the fretboard puzzle.

Let us apply this idea through an example. As illustrated in Figure 15, we want to find the interval from a note on the 5th string to another on the 2nd string, both on the same fret (i.e. interval from the 5th to the 2nd string).

---

[2] This statement begs for being qualified further. Naturally, one or more octaves set a simple and compound interval apart. But on the guitar, playing the 4th or 11th degree of a scale is much the same; in chords, because guitarists often use inversions, a 4th and 11th degree account for the same harmonic function and the distinction belongs to terminology (e.g. sus4, maj add11 chords both contain the 4th degree). You can keep track of the compounds when determining intervals, it just requires a little more brain power!

Intervallic Fretboard – Towards improvising on the Guitar

2- String intervals

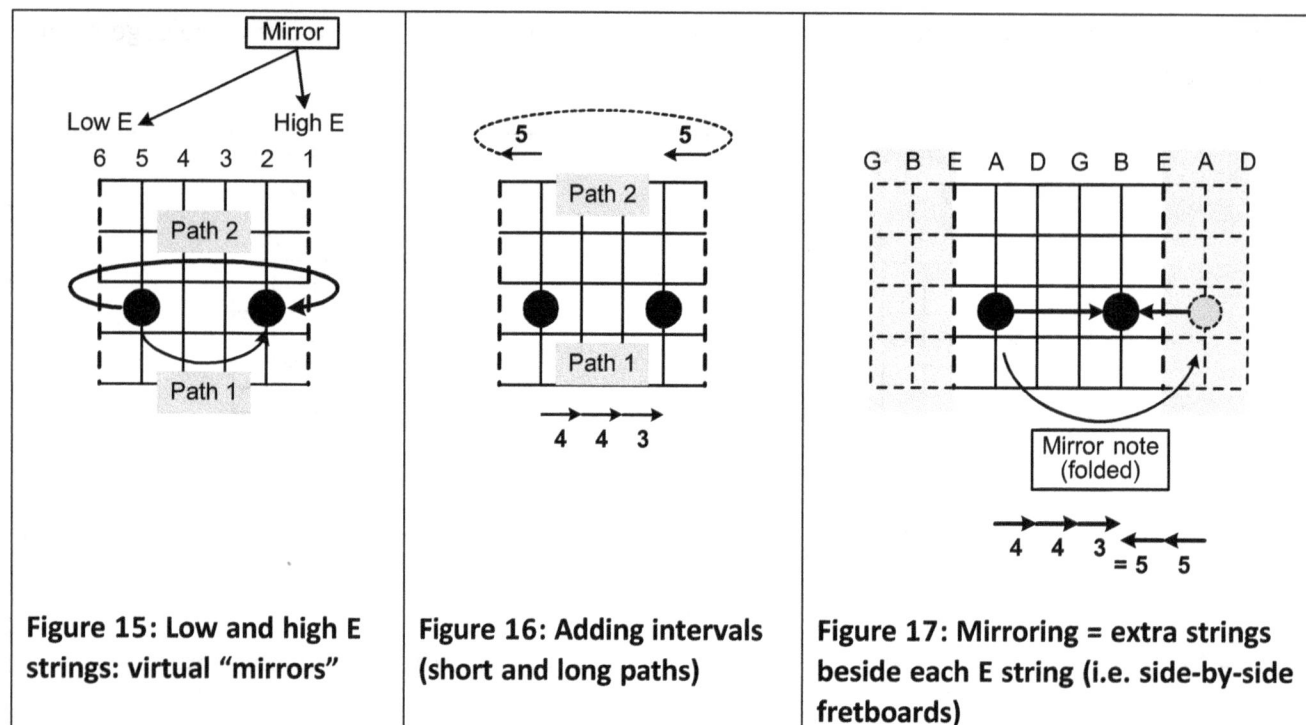

Figure 15: Low and high E strings: virtual "mirrors"

Figure 16: Adding intervals (short and long paths)

Figure 17: Mirroring = extra strings beside each E string (i.e. side-by-side fretboards)

Instead of going up from the 5th to 2nd strings (Path 1), it is far easier to choose the other way, going down from the 5th to the 6th string (virtually the same as the 1st string) and then on to the 2nd string (Path 2).

Long Path 1: 4th+4th+3rd=2nd (same as 3 strings away: 3 string intervals to add)[3]
Short Path 2: 5th+5th=2nd (same as 2 strings away: only 2 string intervals to add)

This brings the 5th and 2nd strings from being 3 strings apart to only 2 strings away. *Literally, there is never a need to look further than 2 strings away to name an interval, thanks to this symmetry.*

---

[3] Some may find it convenient to use an interim reference point for adding intervals: the tritone (half an octave) is a perfect candidate. For example, 4th+4th+3rd=♭7th+3rd=2nd. Referencing 4th+4th back to the tritone, it equals a ♭7th (two half steps short of an octave since a 4th is half a step less than a tritone), which is somewhat more simple to add to a 3rd. Beware that unfortunately, intervals don't add up as in the decimal system (a 5th + 5th is not a 10th but a 9th) – it would have been too good to be true!

2- String intervals

Interval recognition:
Once you are comfortable with that, try intervals from a note to another, not on the same fret, as shown in Figure 18. Your first reaction might be: "Oh dear! That's a lot of strings to add up" (counting string intervals). Not to worry, it boils down to a very short and quick addition – just use the trick of the mirror.

Always look at intervals going up and down the strings (here, it is a $4^{th}=\flat7+5^{th}$ going up and a $5^{th}=4^{th}+2^{nd}$ going down; the sum of an interval and its inversion $4^{th}+5^{th}$=octave is always an octave). The *corner note* in dotted lines in the diagram serves as the intersection point between vertical and horizontal intervals, and can be used as an intermediate step in the overall interval "calculation" (the alternate choice of Figure 21, diagonally opposite, is equally valid). The high E note is mirrored on the low E string in order to avoid adding intervals separating strings 5 to 1 (it's the same as the interval separating strings 5 to 6). This "calculation" should become effortless with time and practise! In fact, eventually, you won't need to calculate intervals so much anymore, you will plainly recognise them by inspection.

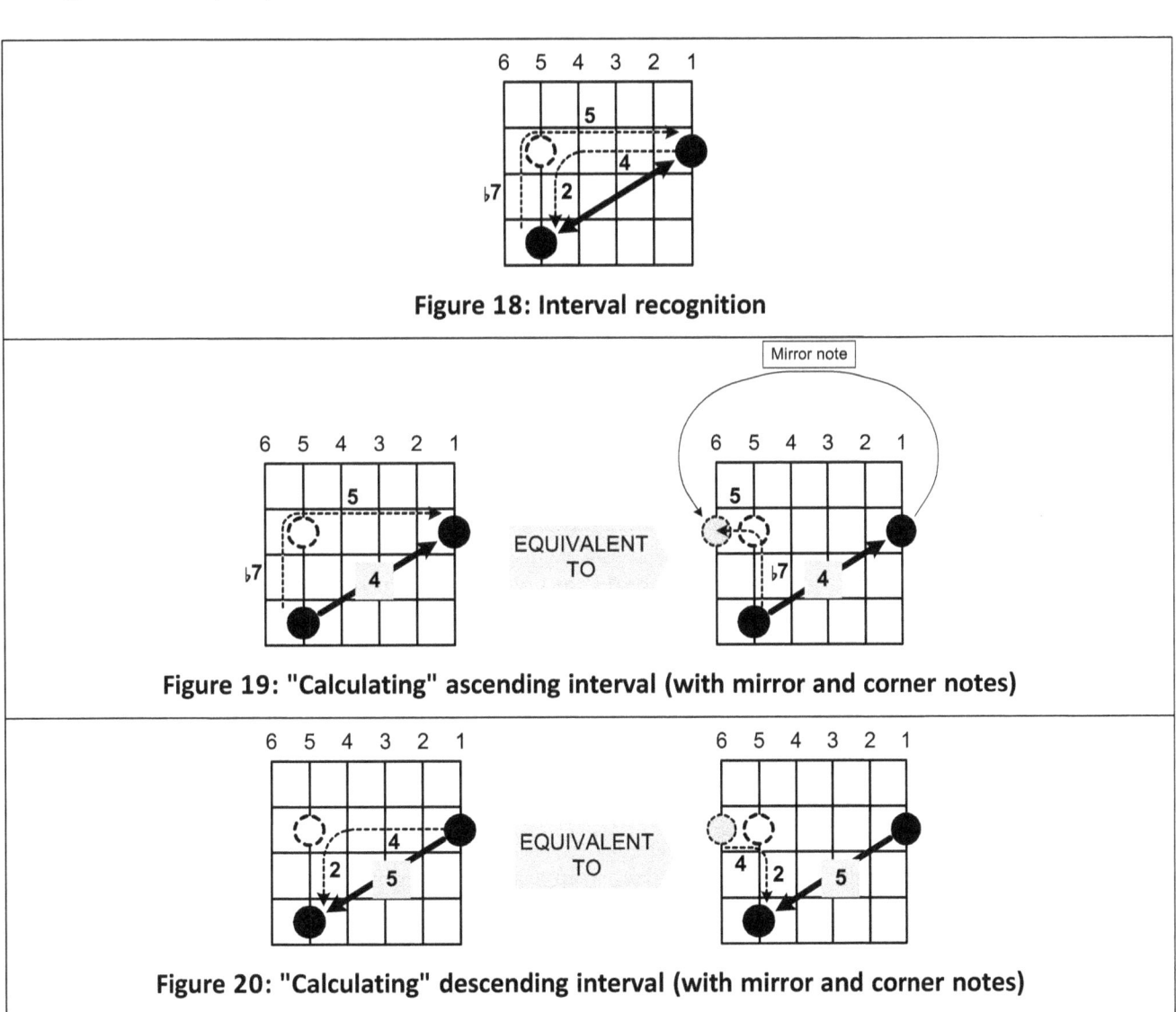

Figure 18: Interval recognition

Figure 19: "Calculating" ascending interval (with mirror and corner notes)

Figure 20: "Calculating" descending interval (with mirror and corner notes)

Put less wordily, this exercise consisted in naming an interval and its inversion. Simply recall the following basic rules when inverting an interval (Chapter 1):

2- String intervals

- Major becomes minor
- Minor becomes major
- Perfect remains perfect
- Augmented becomes diminished and vice versa (or a tritone remains a tritone)

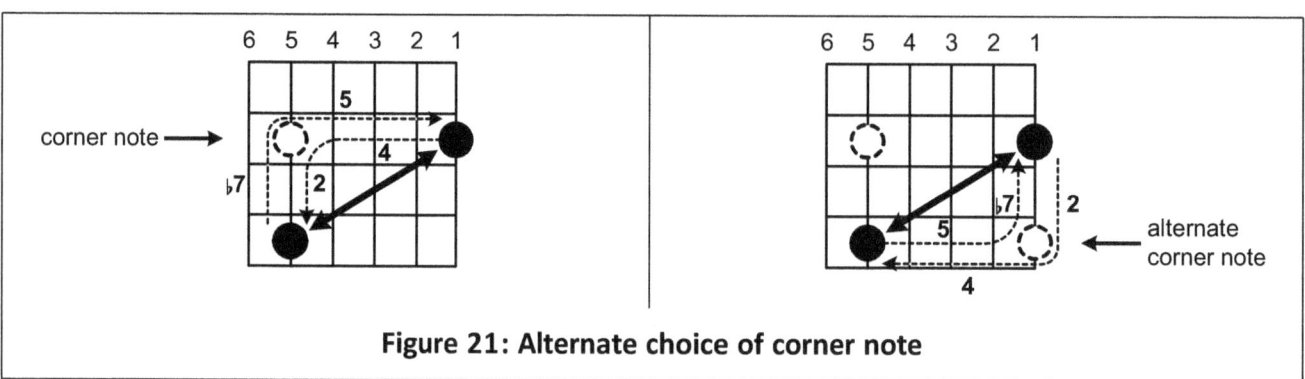

Figure 21: Alternate choice of corner note

Along the same lines, train yourself at recognising wide extensions between strings, such as that in Figure 22 (a minor 2nd is depicted upwards or a major 7th downwards).

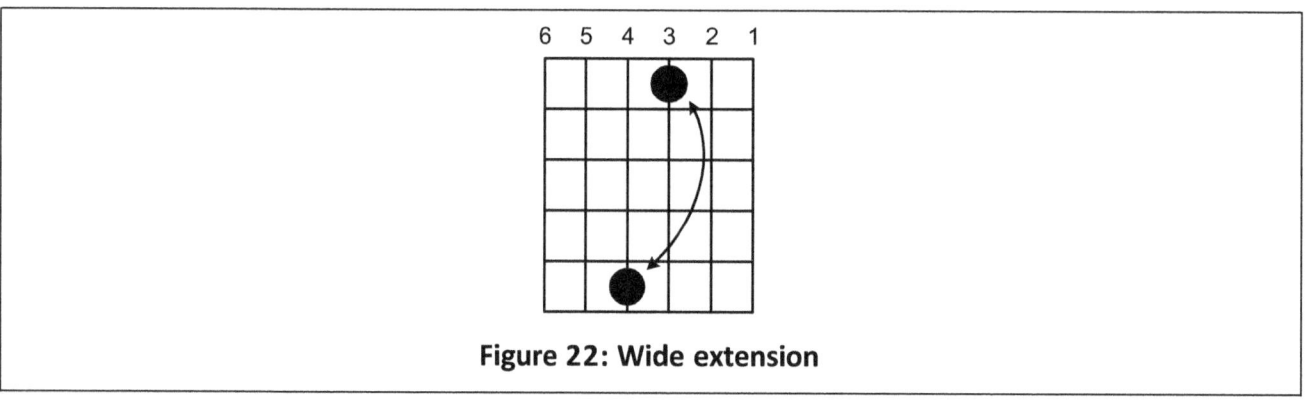

Figure 22: Wide extension

While playing these intervals, it is recommended that you get accustomed to the way each sounds. Appendix A contains a number of intervals on various string pairs and of different qualities. Practise naming those intervals, from the lower to the higher pitch note and vice versa. At first, the steps discussed in the previous paragraphs might be necessary (corner note, mirror note, adding adjacent string intervals). Soon enough though, you will start recognising the intervals at a glance. You can expand the interval diagrams at will, or go through a similar exercise with chords, scale patterns...and name those intervals!

Also, you might try yourself at viewing any two notes as anything but roots or fundamentals, and visualise the interval between them. We will coin this *"non-root intervals"*. For example, view one note as a major 3rd, and the other as a minor 7th (or flat 7th) – as opposed to viewing them as a fundamental and an augmented 4th (or raised 4th). This interval is a tritone, by the way (Figure 23). Gaining awareness in that realm will come in handy in scales, building lines out of sequences (e.g. in 3^{rd}s, 4^{th}s, 6^{th}s), or playing double-stops etc.

2- String intervals

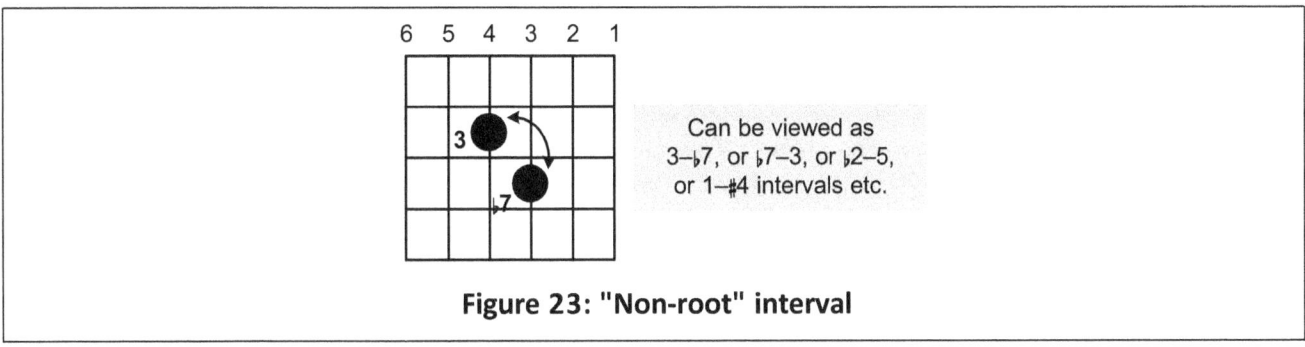

Figure 23: "Non-root" interval

It is worthwhile to use your knowledge of string intervals (and mirroring) to rapidly build a pictorial map of the neck in a given position. For example, in Figure 24, if you choose the fundamental/root (1) on the 5th string, you should not only recognise immediately the 5th below (6th string) and the 4th above (4th string), you should also quickly see that on the same fret, two strings away, there is the ♭7th (3rd string) and that three strings away, there is the natural 2nd. Note that it is straightforward to get to the natural 2nd using the mirroring concept (it virtually is then two strings away from the root/fundamental, instead of three strings away).

Do not attempt to memorise these charts; painstakingly go through the "calculation" steps outlined earlier and let it sink in – it will soon pay off. As you become fluent with intervals on the guitar, this type of fingerboard map will be almost committed to memory.

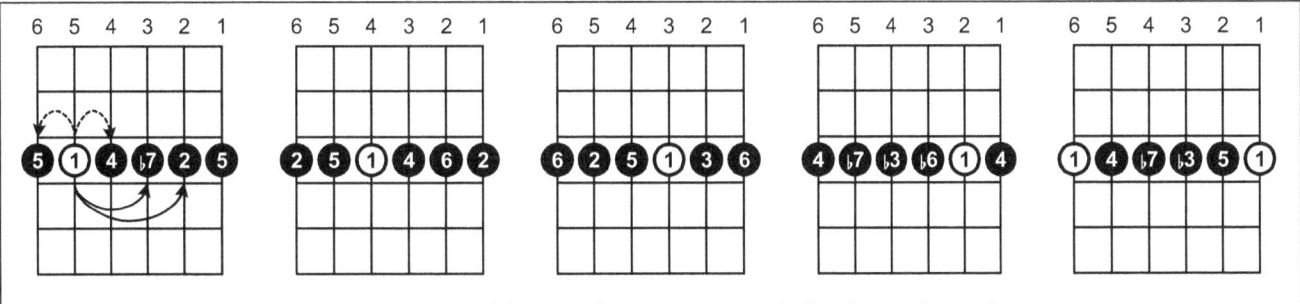

Figure 24: String intervals in one position – pictorial map of the fingerboard

Interval exercises:

An immediate application of intervals is playing them diatonically, either as single notes or double-stops. Being familiar with the harmonisation of the diatonic scale[4], intervals in 3rds and 5ths and even 7ths are straightforward (e.g. in a major scale, all the 5ths are perfect except for that built on the leading tone which is diminished). 2nds are trivial as they consist merely of successive notes of the scale.

Intervals in 4ths and 6ths however, appear to be trickier at first, as diatonic harmonisation does not typically include those intervals in any chord (e.g. what is the quality of a diatonic sixth built on the 2nd degree G of the F major scale?). A mnemonic device is to treat the diatonic 4th and 6th as

---

[4] In traditional harmony, chords are built by stacking intervals of a 3rd. For example, we know that the II chord of the major scale is a minor triad (1–♭3–5) or a minor 7th chord (1–♭3–5–♭7). Thus giving the quality of the 3rd, 5th, and 7th intervals formed from the 2nd degree of the major scale.

2- String intervals

diatonic 5th and 3rd, respectively, only with an inversion. A simple way to bring those two intervals into familiar territory!

Thus, the focus would be on the diatonic movement of the 4th and 6th notes themselves, when we play those intervals, rather than the "root" of each interval (Figure 25, Figure 26).

Once again, the guiding principle is simplicity – there is no need to learn the same thing several times. *As we just saw, knowledge of the quality of the 4th and 6th is no more than knowledge of the quality of the 5th and 3rd, interpreted differently.*

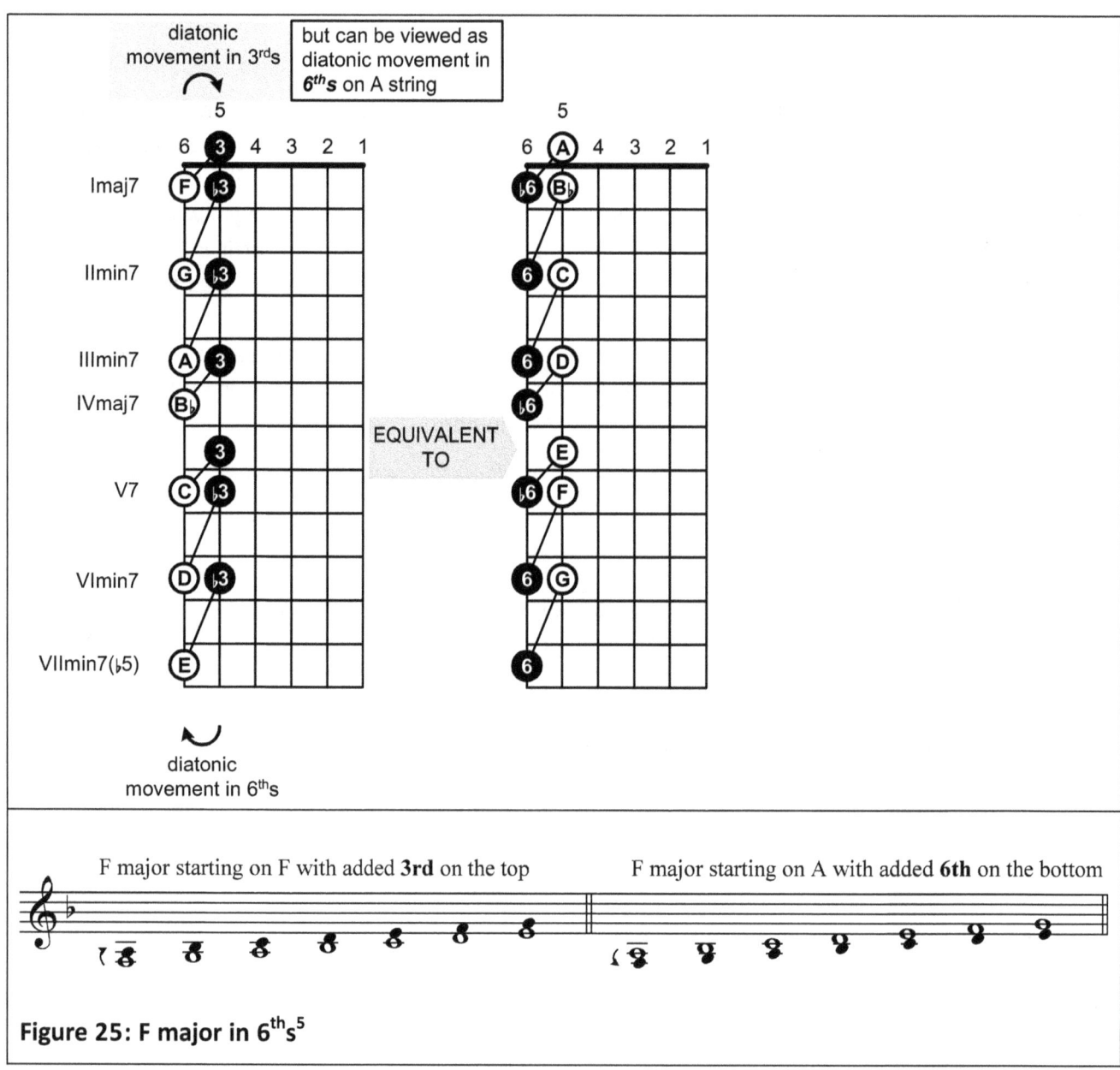

Figure 25: F major in 6ths[5]

---

[5] Due to the convention adopted in Chapter 1 (section "Inversion"). Otherwise, it would be named F major in ascending 3rds and F major in descending 3rds, instead of F major in 3rds and F major in 6ths, respectively. Remember, since the harmonic function of the notes is of interest, we are doing away with octave displacement that an inversion would incur. It is simply a matter of semantics.

Intervallic Fretboard – Towards improvising on the Guitar

2- String intervals

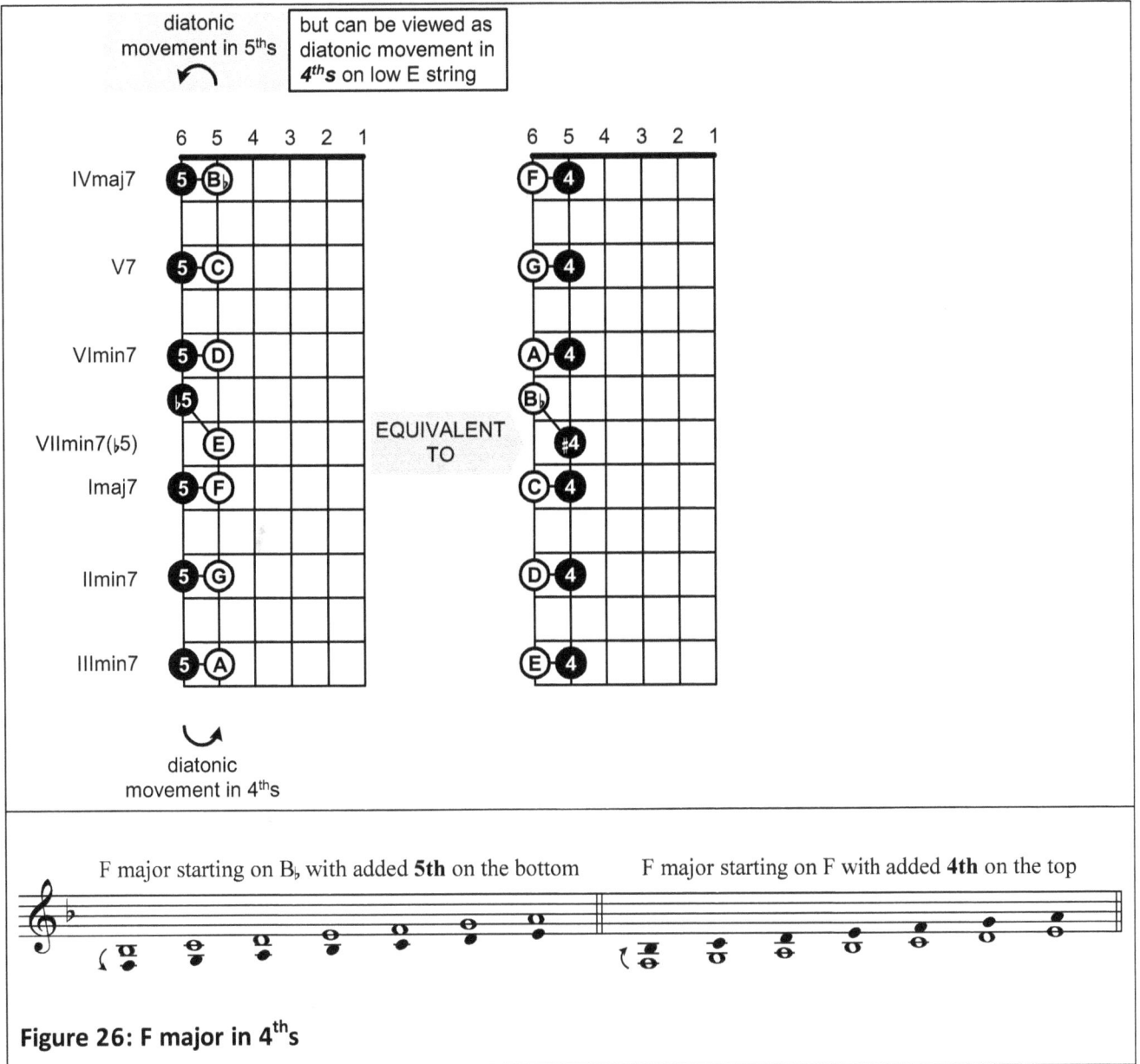

Figure 26: F major in 4ths

The following examples show diatonic interval playing (sometimes called interval scales). Play them ascending, as notated, and descending. You can also practise the inversion tip (i.e. view intervals in 6ths as intervals in 3rds with an inversion). For the first example in C Mixolydian (Example 1), the interval-based notation shows two ways of thinking: the first moves through the mode using non-root intervals in 4ths (1–4, 2–5, 3–6, 4–♭7 etc.), the other interprets the 4ths as 5ths (the 5th being the lower note in pitch in the interval), while the reference tone below the staff moves through the C Mixolydian scale.
The same examples can also be played as sequences.

Note: The notation staff labelled "IVL" is explained in Appendix B titled "Interval-based notation system". Although your intuition may help you make sense out of this curious notation, it is recommended that you read Appendix B in conjunction with this chapter.

Example 1: C Mixolydian mode in 4ths

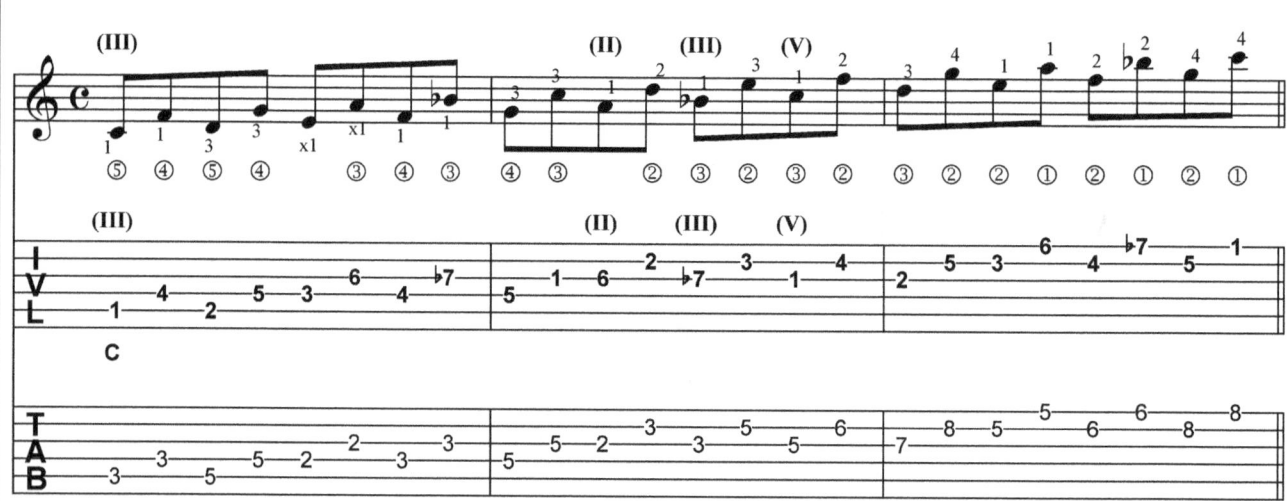

Below: same but viewed in intervals of 5ths (ascending the Mixolydian mode with the 5th degree note of the interval in the bottom and the root in the top; the reference tone changes with each interval and ascends the C Mixolydian mode).

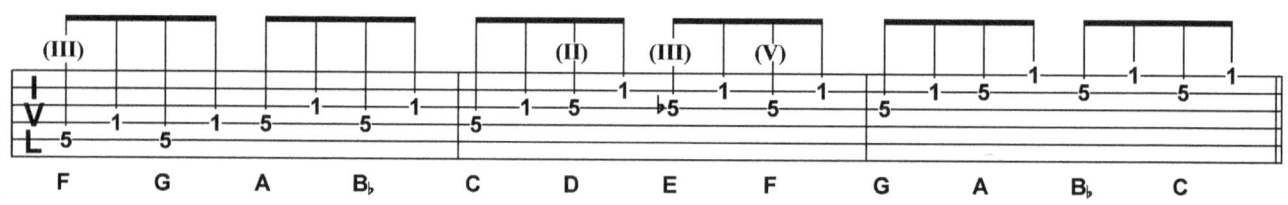

Example 2: G (natural) minor scale in 6ths

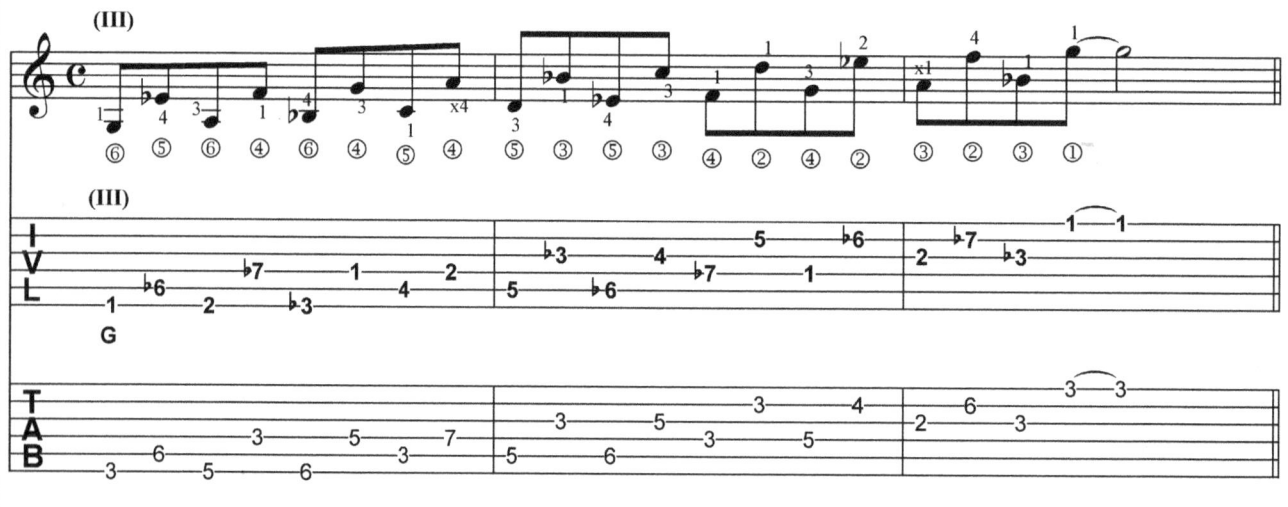

2- String intervals

Example 3: A harmonic minor scale in 7ths

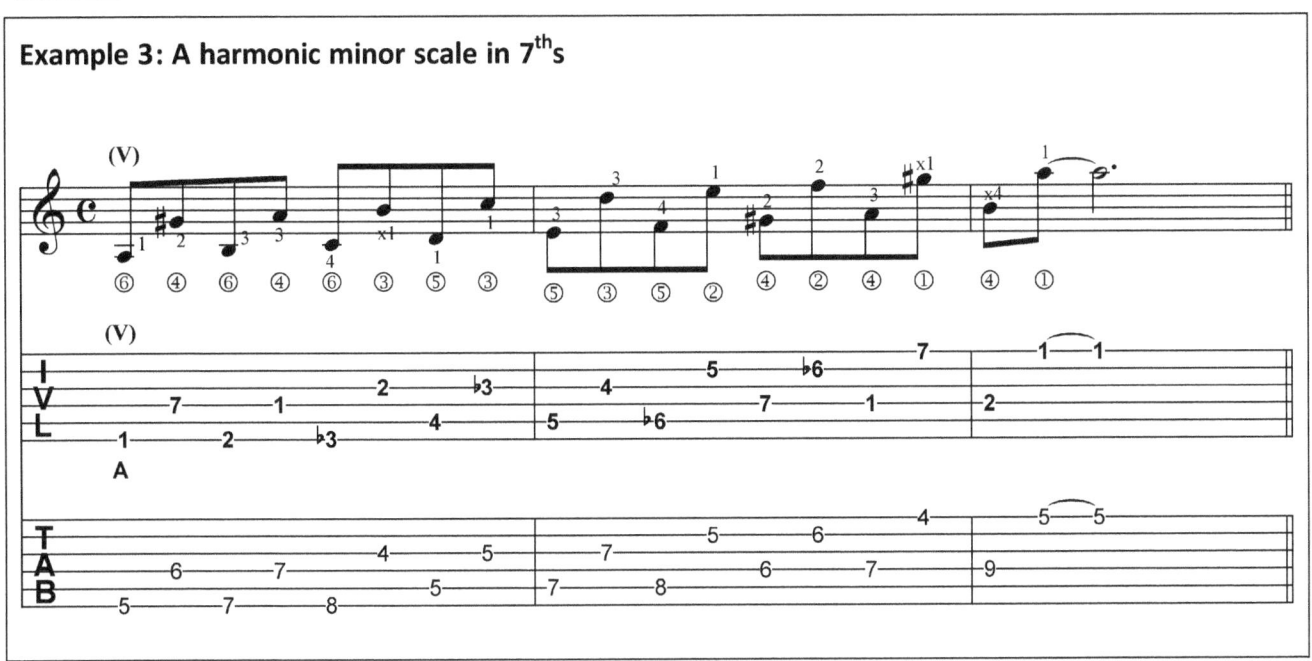

Example 4 scrolls through the B pentatonic minor scale followed by the B blues scale, while holding down one note (pedal tone: ♭3rd then ♭7th). All the intervals within those two scales are played.

Example 4: B pentatonic minor and B blues scales with pedal tone (♭3rd and ♭7th)

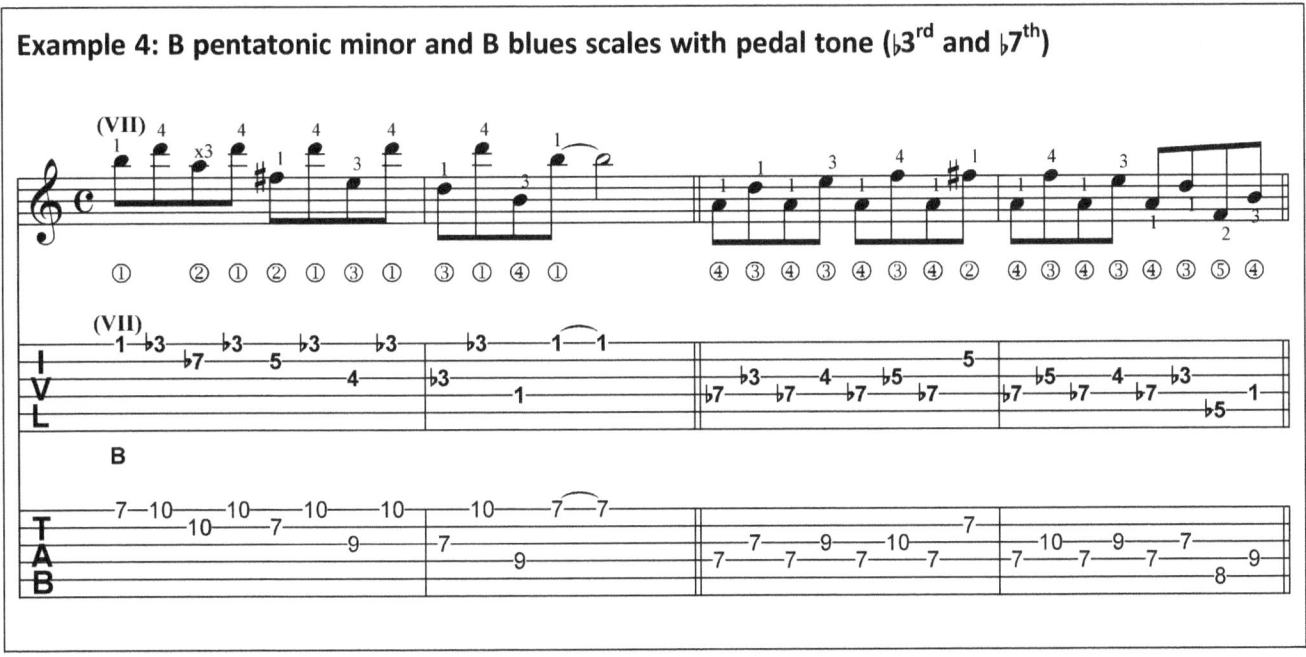

The next few examples show intervals played as double-stops across the neck and string sets, building melodic ideas. These intervals are diatonic to a particular scale, and require that you keep track of your whereabouts within that scale, like the previous examples.

The last exercise (Example 7) mixes different interval qualities, all drawn from E major. The thought process followed in writing this exercise was to take a melodic idea (the voice with stems down) and add various diatonic intervals to each note (the voice with stems up). Most of the melodic idea

2- String intervals

constitutes the bottom note of the intervals in this case, but one should develop equal facility adding intervals on the bottom and on the top of a given note.

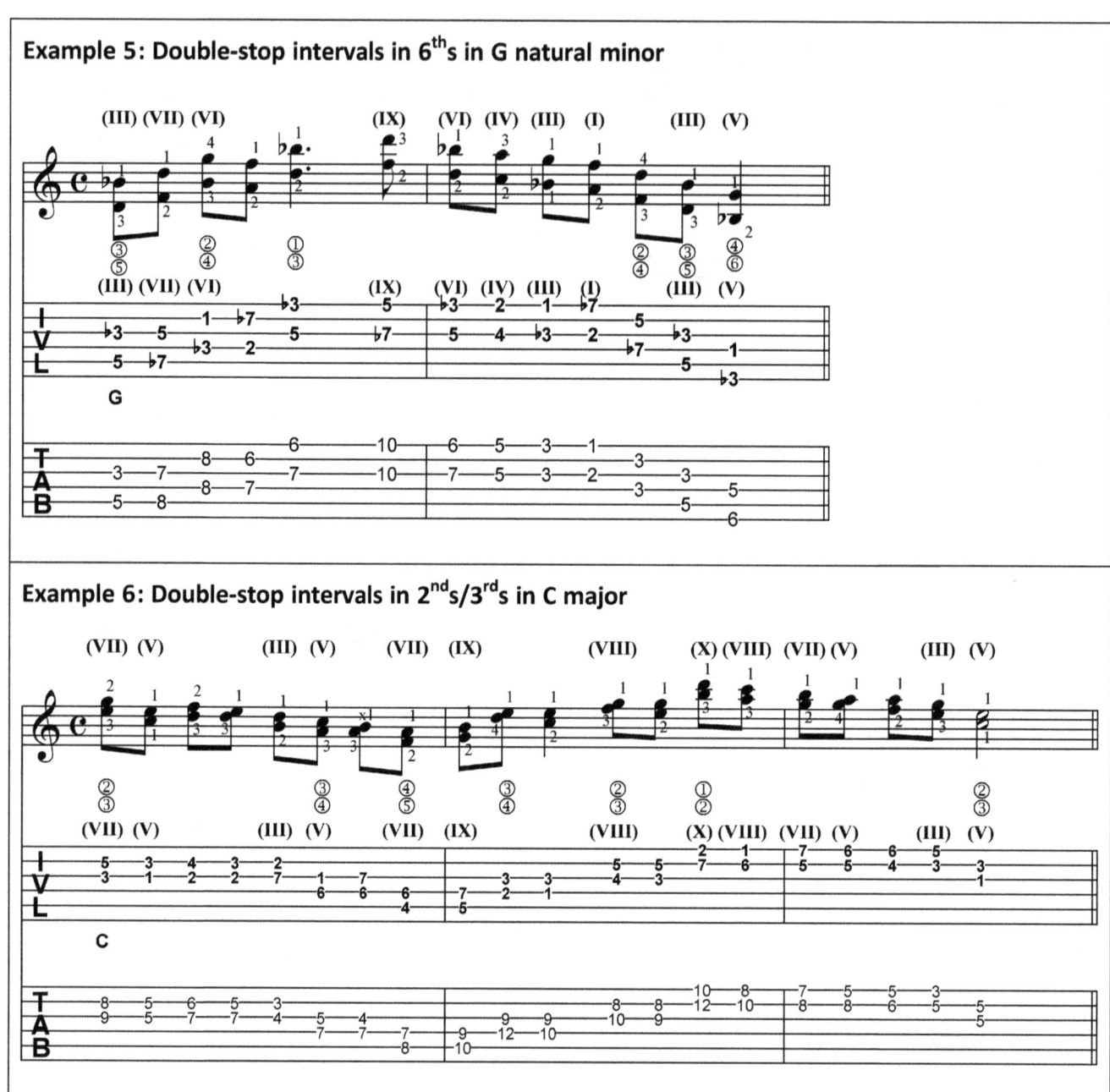

Example 5: Double-stop intervals in 6ths in G natural minor

Example 6: Double-stop intervals in 2nds/3rds in C major

2- String intervals

Example 7: Double-stops mixing intervals in E major

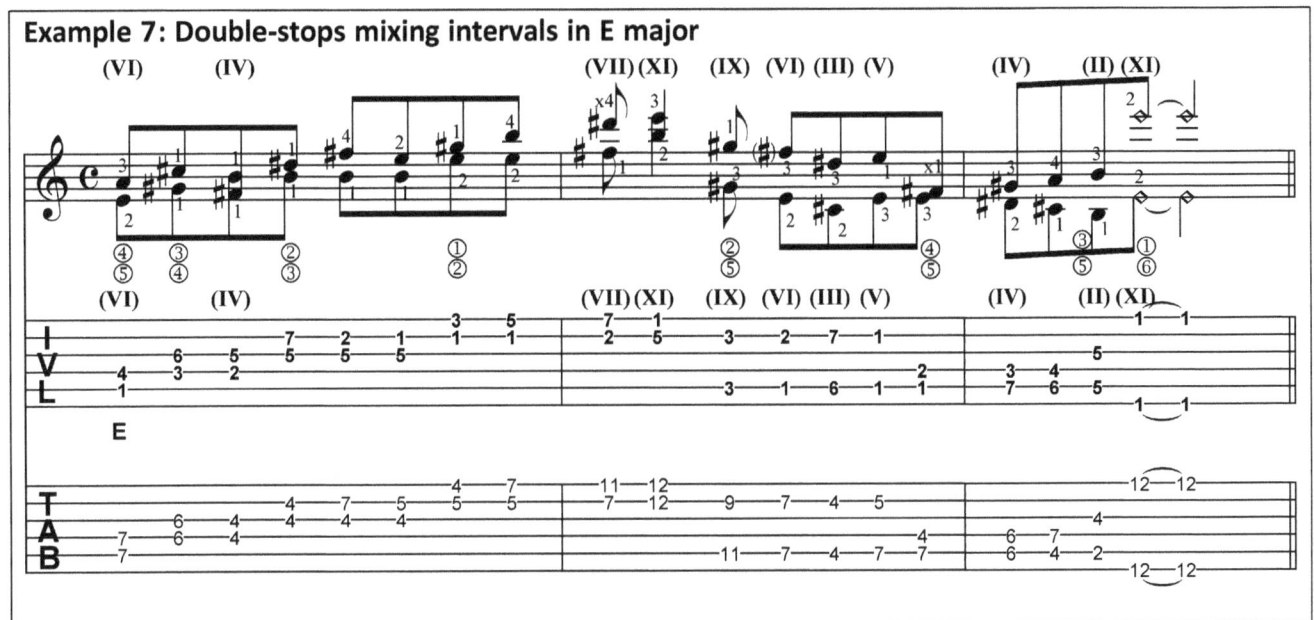

Stacking intervals: triads...and beyond

Anticipating the following chapter, the next stage in developing interval fluency is to put our newly acquired knowledge of adjacent string intervals to work, in the context of the most elementary chord form: the triad. Illustrating the 2–3 string shift by the same token, we now take a more systematic approach with triads across the neck, exploring the forms a given voicing takes as we move along the neck to higher registers (horizontally) and across strings (vertically).

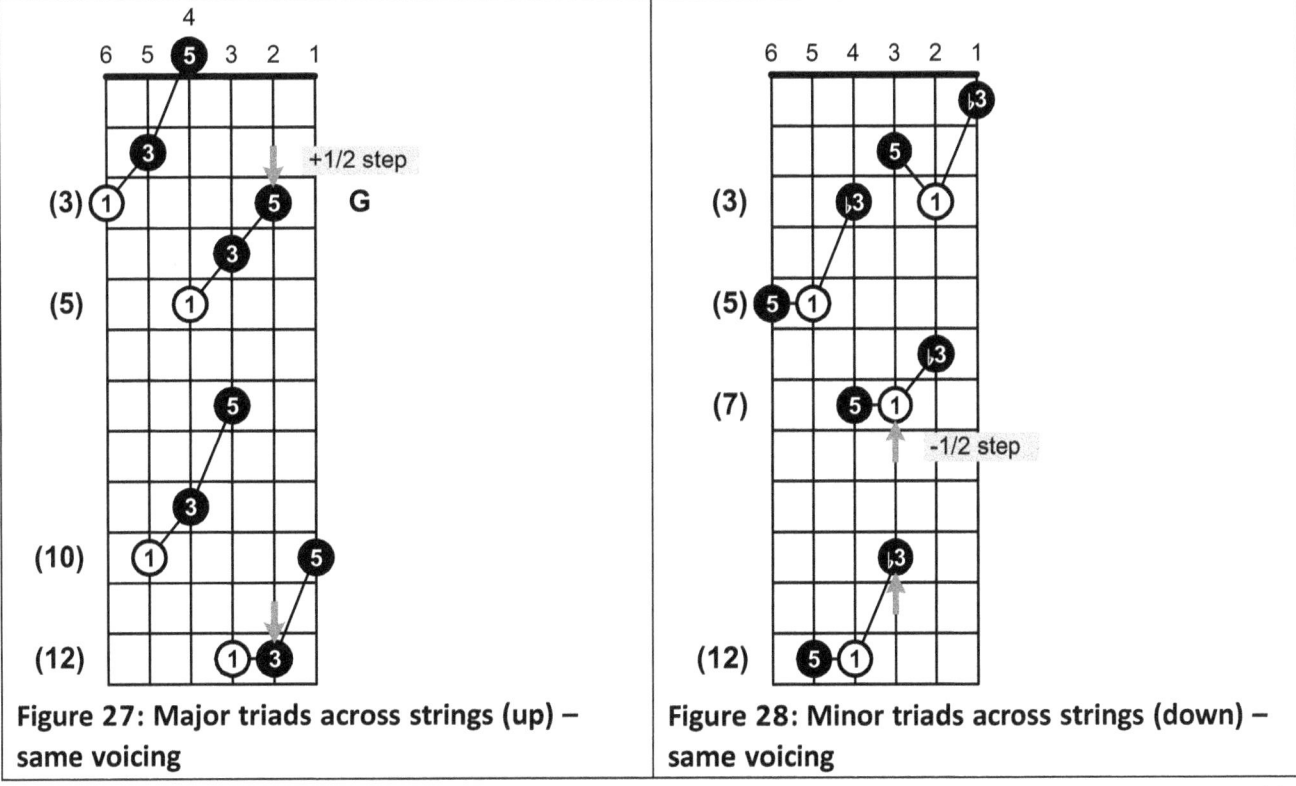

Figure 27: Major triads across strings (up) – same voicing

Figure 28: Minor triads across strings (down) – same voicing

Intervallic Fretboard – Towards improvising on the Guitar

2- String intervals

The diagram in Figure 27 shows a G major triad in the same voicing over 3 strings in closed-form[6], across all four 3-string closed string sets. Pay close attention to the 3rd and 5th of the triad as the major triads in Figure 27 move up the strings. When the root of the triad moves from string 5 to 4, the 5th makes the jump from 3rd to 2nd string, and is pushed one fret closer towards the remainder body of the triad (compare the shape of the G triad in 5th position to those in 3rd and 10th positions). The same thing occurs in the final G triad in 12th position where the 3rd has now crossed the 3rd string to the 2nd string and is pushed one fret forward.

Figure 28 displays the same idea only with D minor triads this time, and we look at it moving down the strings, hence crossing from the 2nd to the 3rd string.

This shift and how it can be visually taken advantage of is further exemplified through Figure 29, where a G7 chord is moved up one string (one string set) at a time, keeping the same voicing. As the chord name goes through the cycle of fourths, its quality and voicing are kept unchanged, as long as the 2–3 string shift is respected. You may recognise dominant chord shapes you already know. In a later chapter on 7th chords, you will be able to repeat this process at length.

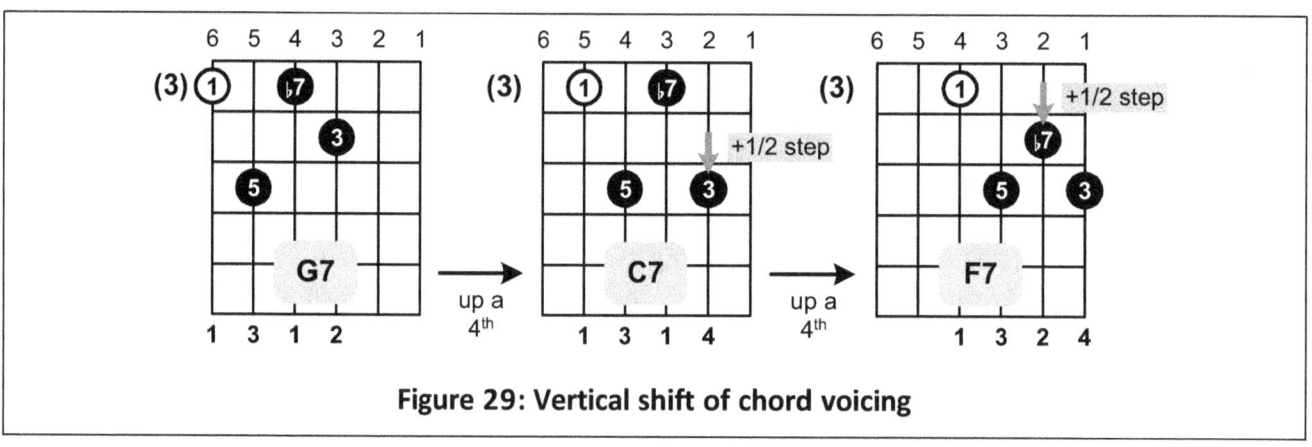

Figure 29: Vertical shift of chord voicing

Although you cannot get around seeing the shapes that these triads form, you should see the intervals first, the shapes second. In other words, if you just take away from this exercise the visual shapes and not the intervals, you are getting shortchanged (the truth is you are being lazy: go back and focus on the intervals/chord tones!).

Practise other triads (minor, diminished, augmented, suspended etc.) and chords, following the same approach, while focusing on intervals, more so than shapes. You may also want to develop 2 or 3-note single string motifs and move them up and down the strings. Triads are a great way to become fluent with 3rd, 5th, 3rd–5th (i.e. minor 3rd) intervals etc.

For example, play multi-octave scales and arpeggios in the same position or diagonally on the neck (back and forth). Midway through, change scales or arpeggios, gradually increasing velocity (Example 8). Those can make for great picking exercises too (alternate, sweep, or economy). One of the objectives is to be able to think intervals in the "long run", i.e. long lines and across the entire neck, and being able to connect lines, without getting lost on the fretboard. Another example,

---

[6] Closed-form chord: a chord where each note is on adjacent strings.
Open-form chord: a chord where one or more notes are not on adjacent strings.

2- String intervals

building on stacking intervals or triads, is an arpeggiated chord (Example 9). Do not memorise this shape but aim for reproducing it or segments of it by "seeing" the intervals on the fretboard.

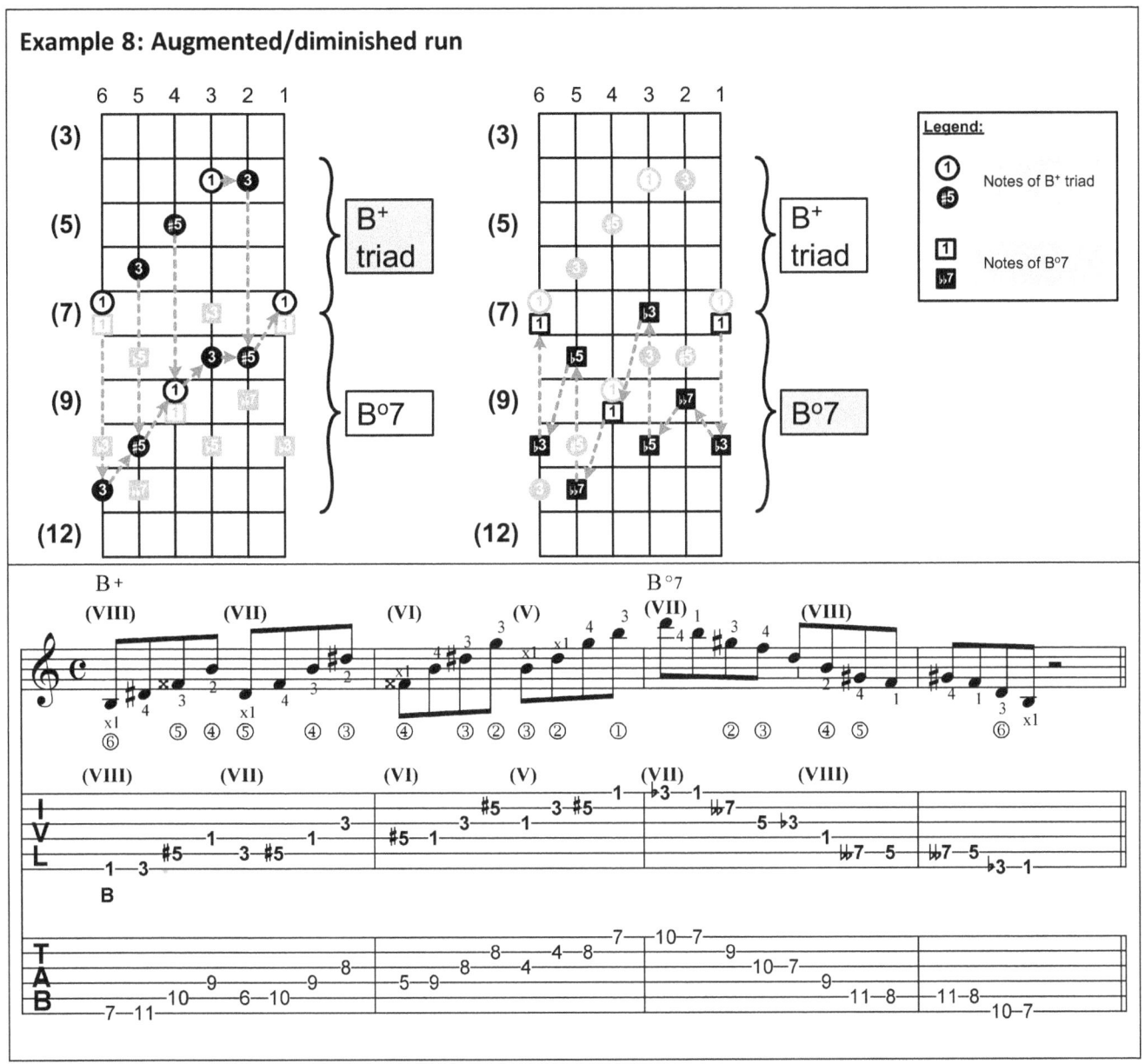

Example 8: Augmented/diminished run

2- String intervals

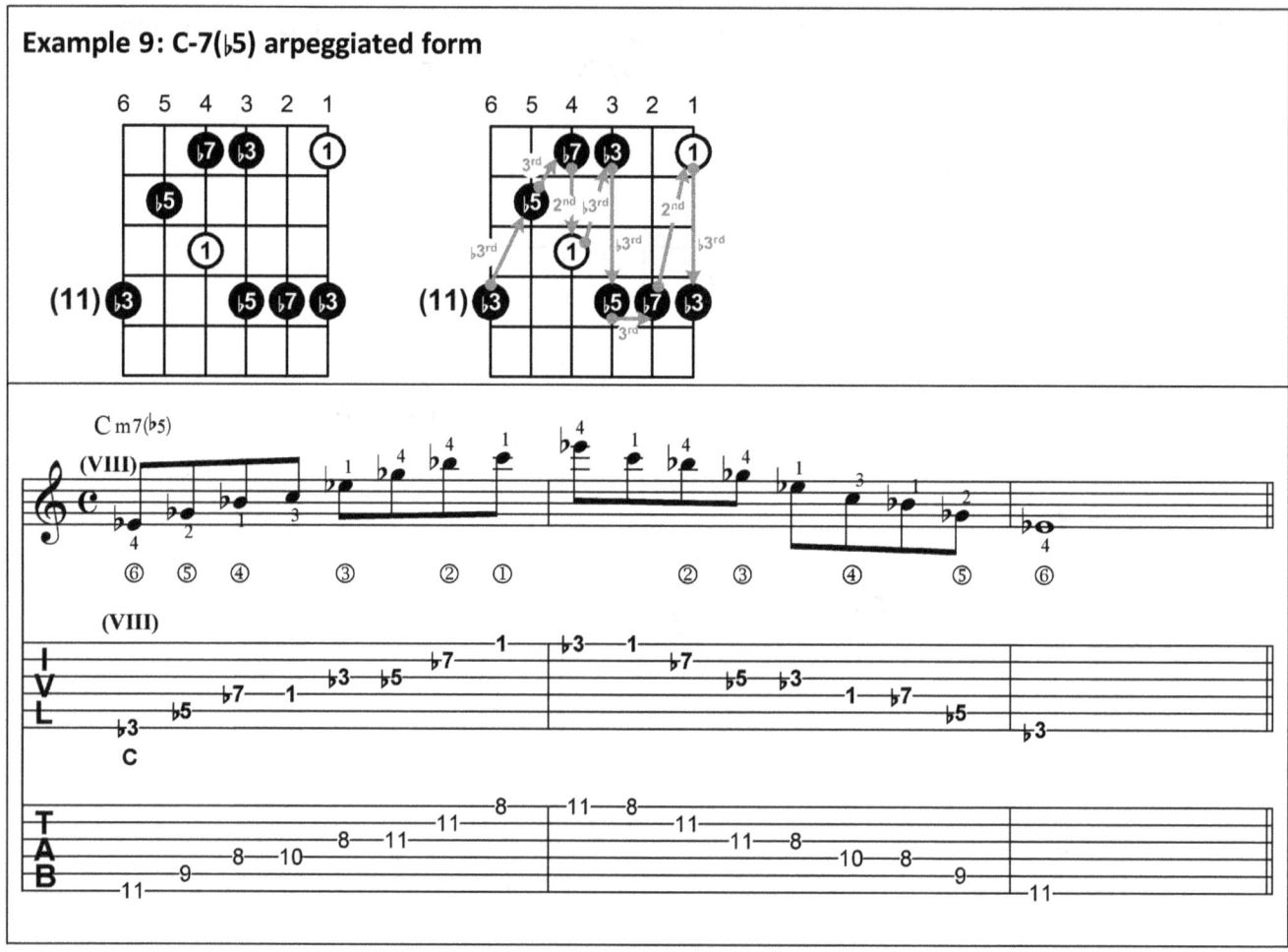

Example 9: C-7(♭5) arpeggiated form

Along the same lines, a good exercise is to practise arpeggios across the neck. Example 10 illustrates this idea by playing connected 7th arpeggios diatonically over each degree of the B♭ major scale, horizontally up the neck. The difficulty resides not only in building the 7th arpeggios stacking up 3rds (major and minor), but also in keeping track of the diatonic movement from one scale degree to the next (i.e. situating yourself within the B♭ major scale). Also note the smooth connection from one arpeggio to the next: the root of the current arpeggio becomes the 7th of the following arpeggio. Example 11 is the same exercise only played in one unique position this time (7th position). This demonstrates the many possibilities of the guitar fingerboard.

2- String intervals

Example 10: Arpeggios in 7ths of B♭ major across the neck

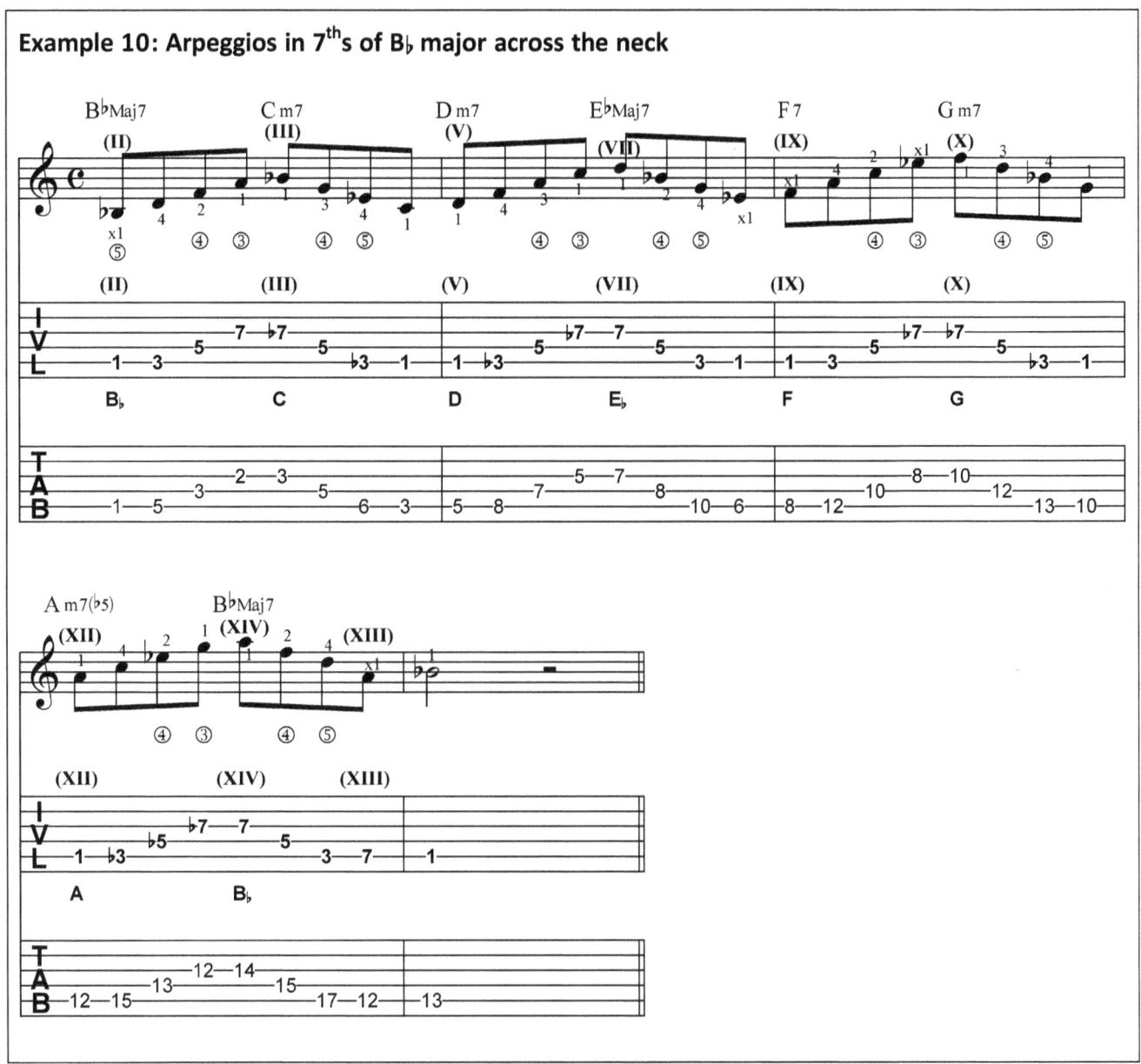

2- String intervals

Example 11: Same exercise in one position only (7th position)

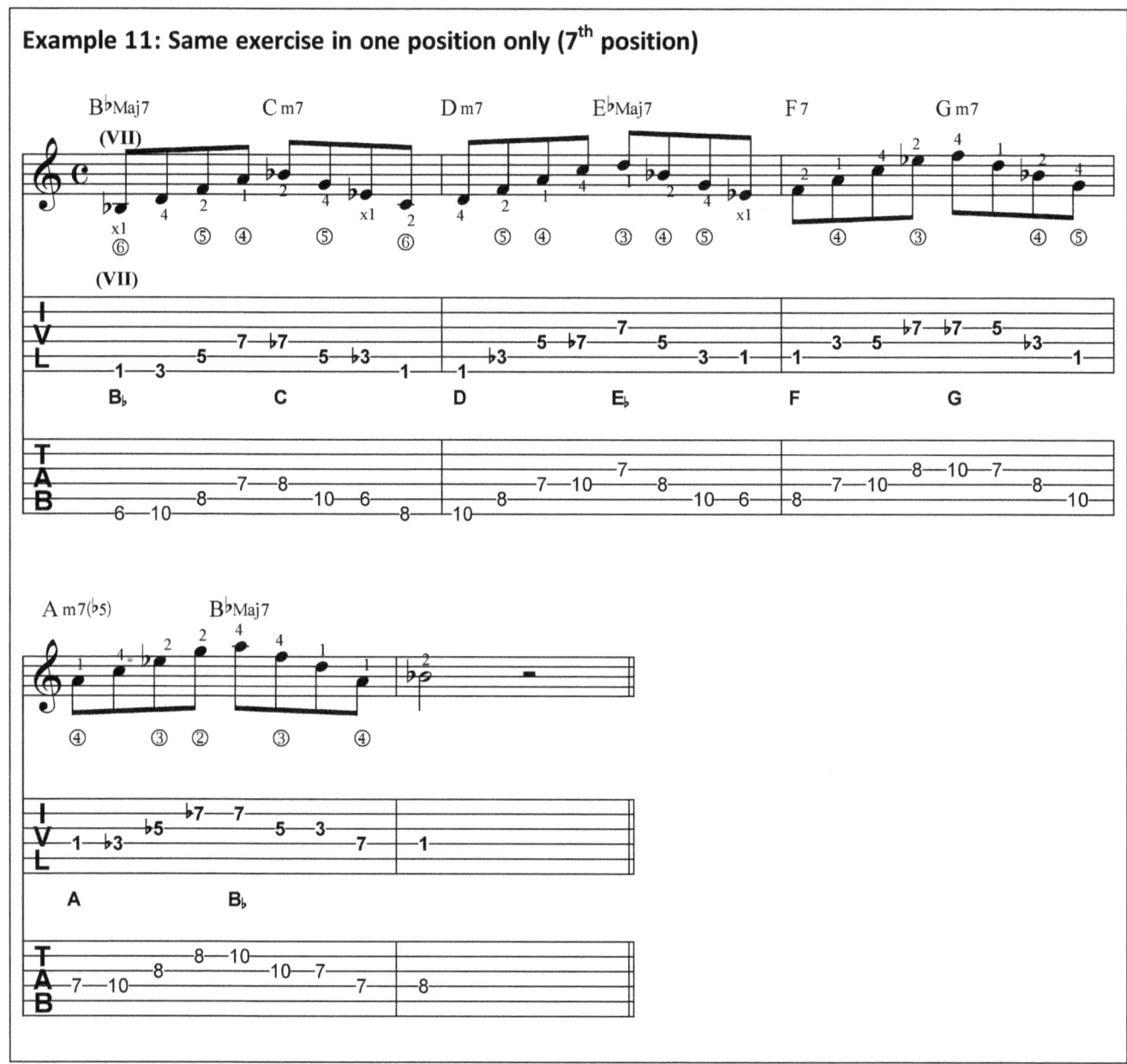

With tenacity, and the exercises hinted at in this section, intervals will start popping up and your vision of the fretboard will take on a whole new meaning.

3 Chords revisited: exploiting tonal distance

n the heels of the various representations and usage of intervals as basic building blocks described in Chapter 2, this section focuses on applying those primitive blocks to build the more complex structures that are chords.

Chord tone and scale tone movement of chords – triads and 7th chords

Many musicians tend to classify chords into three categories: *major*, *minor* and *dominant*. This greatly simplifies how to approach a song and its harmonic progression, especially when it comes to improvising over it.

It is therefore a necessity to master major and minor triads, and all three types of 7th chords across the neck (major, minor, dominant). Those give access to a number of voicings that can be easily morphed into more elaborate chords (extended, altered etc.), by moving notes around or adding/removing notes. This can only be done by not only knowing the chord shapes, but also the function of each note within the chord: an intervallic approach is thereby essential.

While learning these 3 and 4-note chords, recognise the shapes that can be easily pictured when applying the 2–3 string shift. Also observe how moving one note by half a step changes the quality of the chord from maj7 to dom7 to min7.

The chords in a row are shown by moving each chord tone to the next tone in their make-up, i.e. in a major 7th chord, as the chord moves to the next position up the neck, 3rd goes to 5th, 5th goes to 7th, 7th goes to Root etc. We will otherwise name this approach: <u>chord tone movement of chords (also called **_voice leading_**)</u>.

Another perspective would be to change chords each time as the chord moves to the next scale degree, for instance by harmonising a scale on a particular string set (e.g. Figure 38). In Figure 38, F-(1–5–♭3) becomes G° (2–♭6–4) where each note in the chord moves up to the next note in the F-harmonic minor scale, i.e. Root goes to 2nd, 5th goes to ♭6th, ♭3rd goes to 4th and so on. We will refer to this latter approach as <u>scale tone movement of chords (also named **_chord scale_**)</u>. All are worthwhile exercises.

All combinations of string sets are not provided, as some tend to sound muddy or have unfriendly fingerings, but they can be explored as an exercise. Rather than a catalogue, we merely intend the following chords to paint the general idea at work.

<u>Chord tone movement of chords:</u>

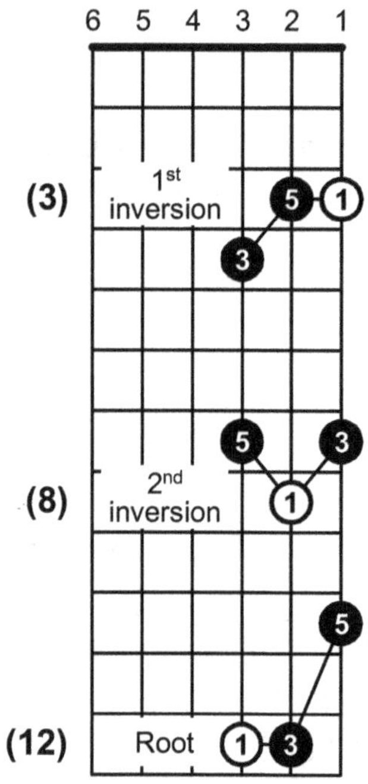

3- Chords revisited: exploiting tonal distance

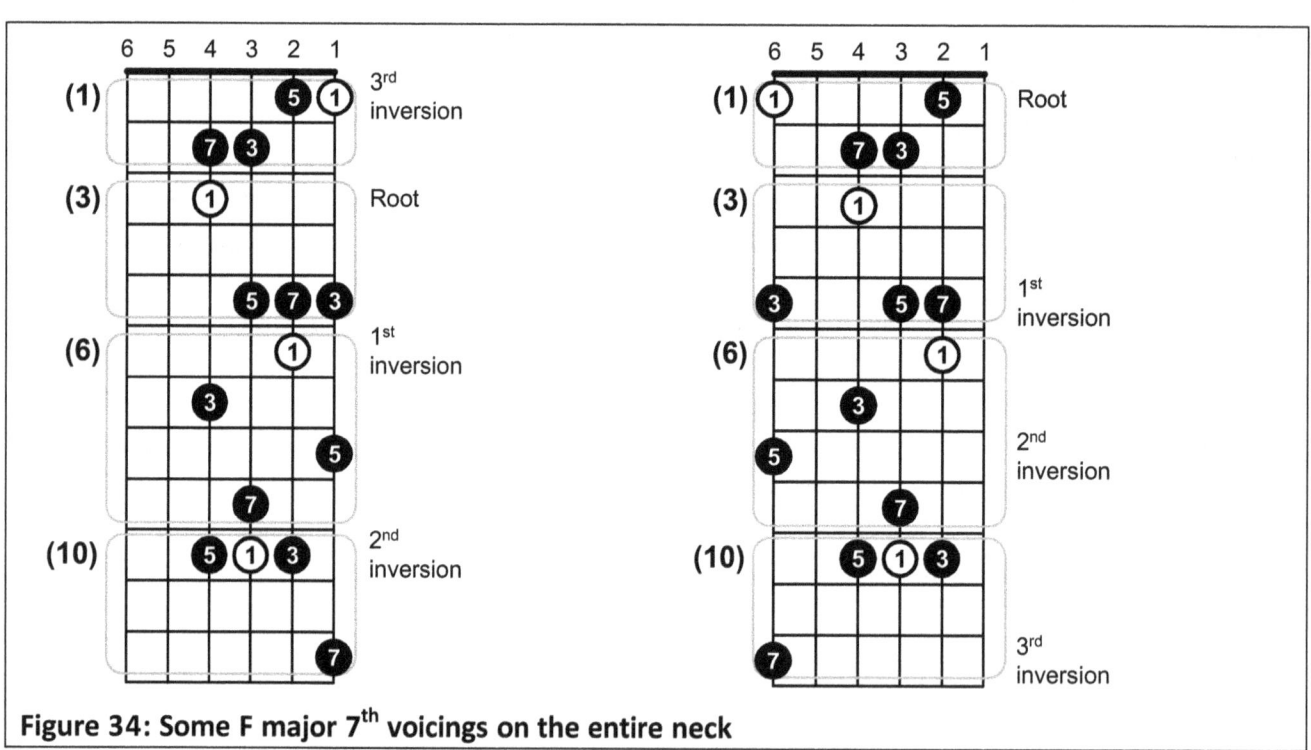

Figure 30: Strings 3-2-1 closed-form G major triad

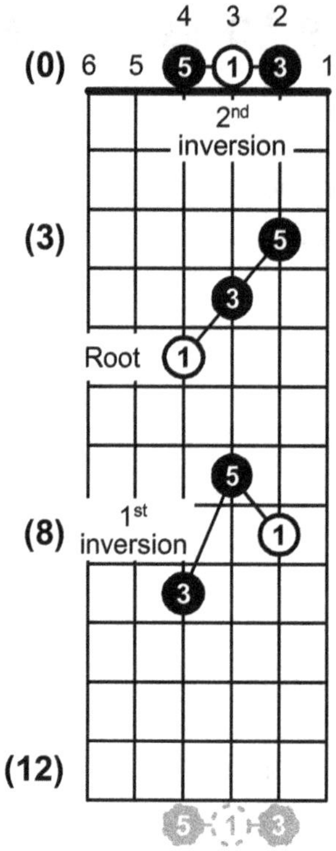

Figure 31: Strings 4-3-2 closed-form G major triad

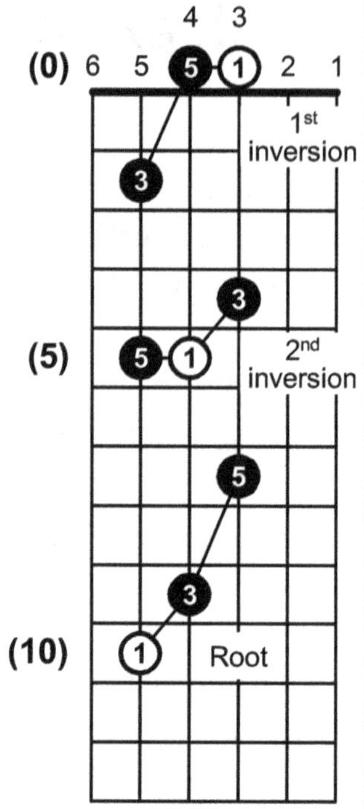

Figure 32: Strings 5-4-3 closed-form G major triad

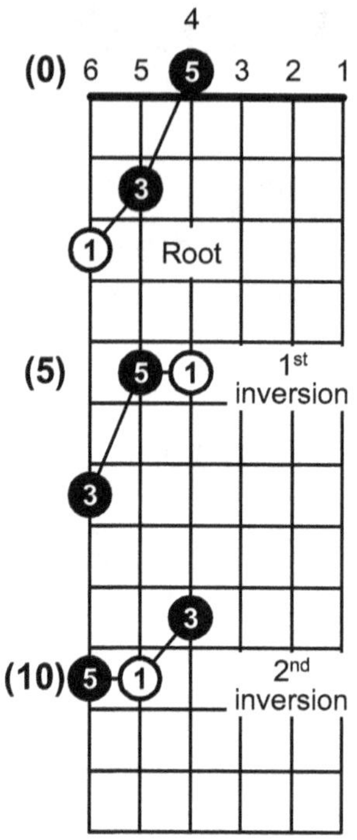

Figure 33: Strings 6-5-4 closed-form G major triad

Figure 34: Some F major 7th voicings on the entire neck

3- Chords revisited: exploiting tonal distance

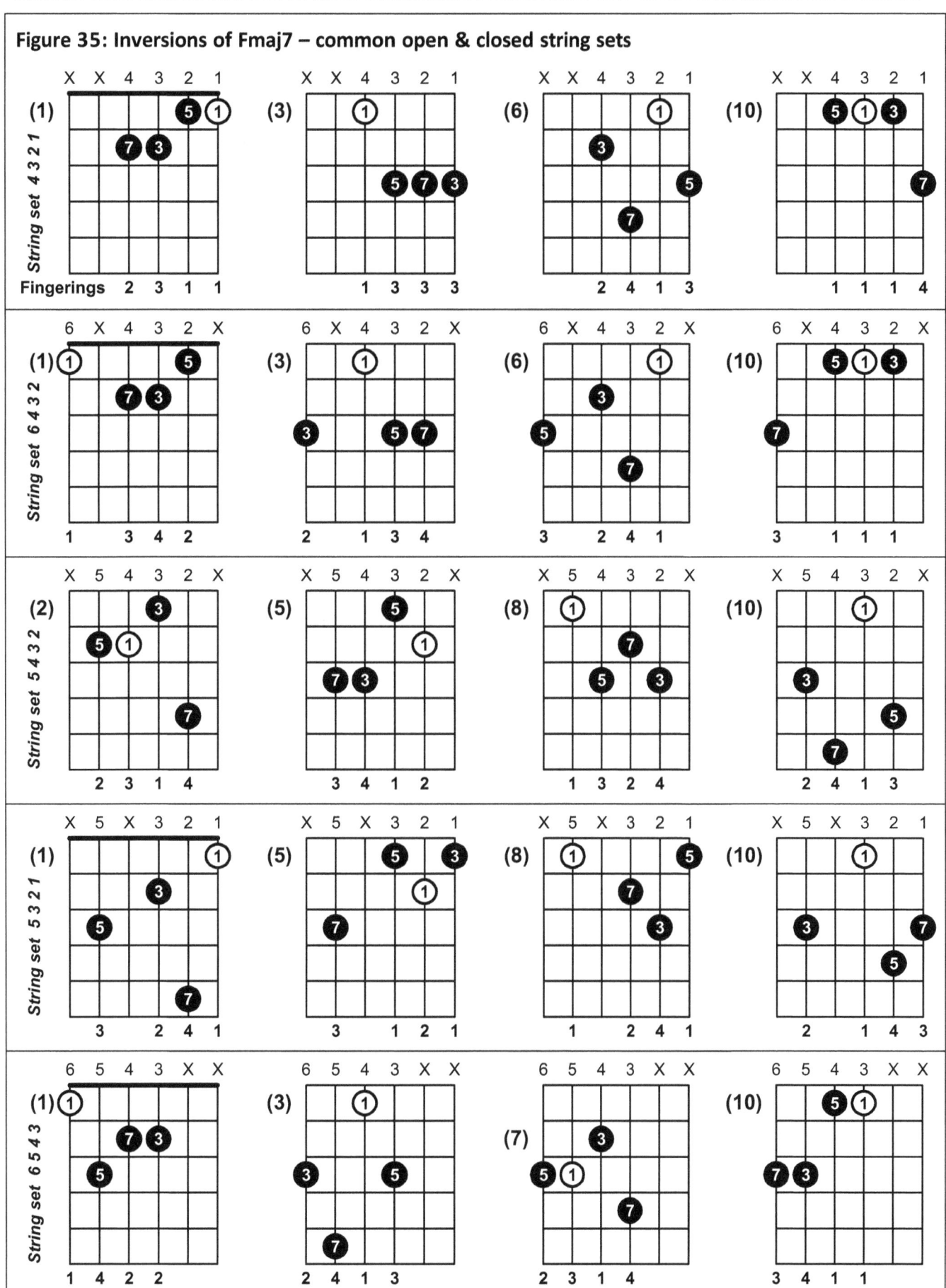

Figure 35: Inversions of Fmaj7 – common open & closed string sets

3- Chords revisited: exploiting tonal distance

Figure 36: Inversions of F7 – common open & closed string sets

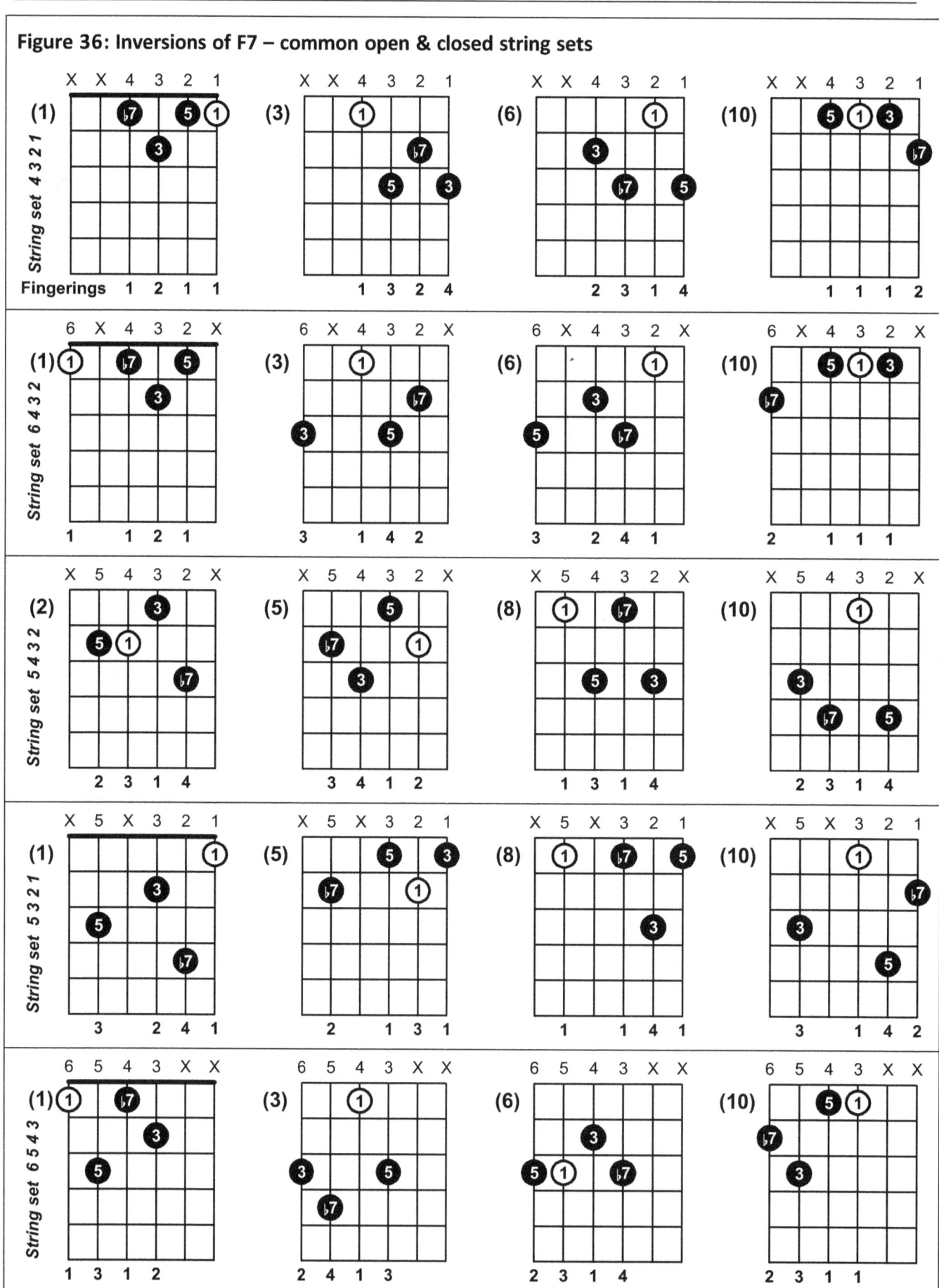

Intervallic Fretboard – Towards improvising on the Guitar

3- Chords revisited: exploiting tonal distance

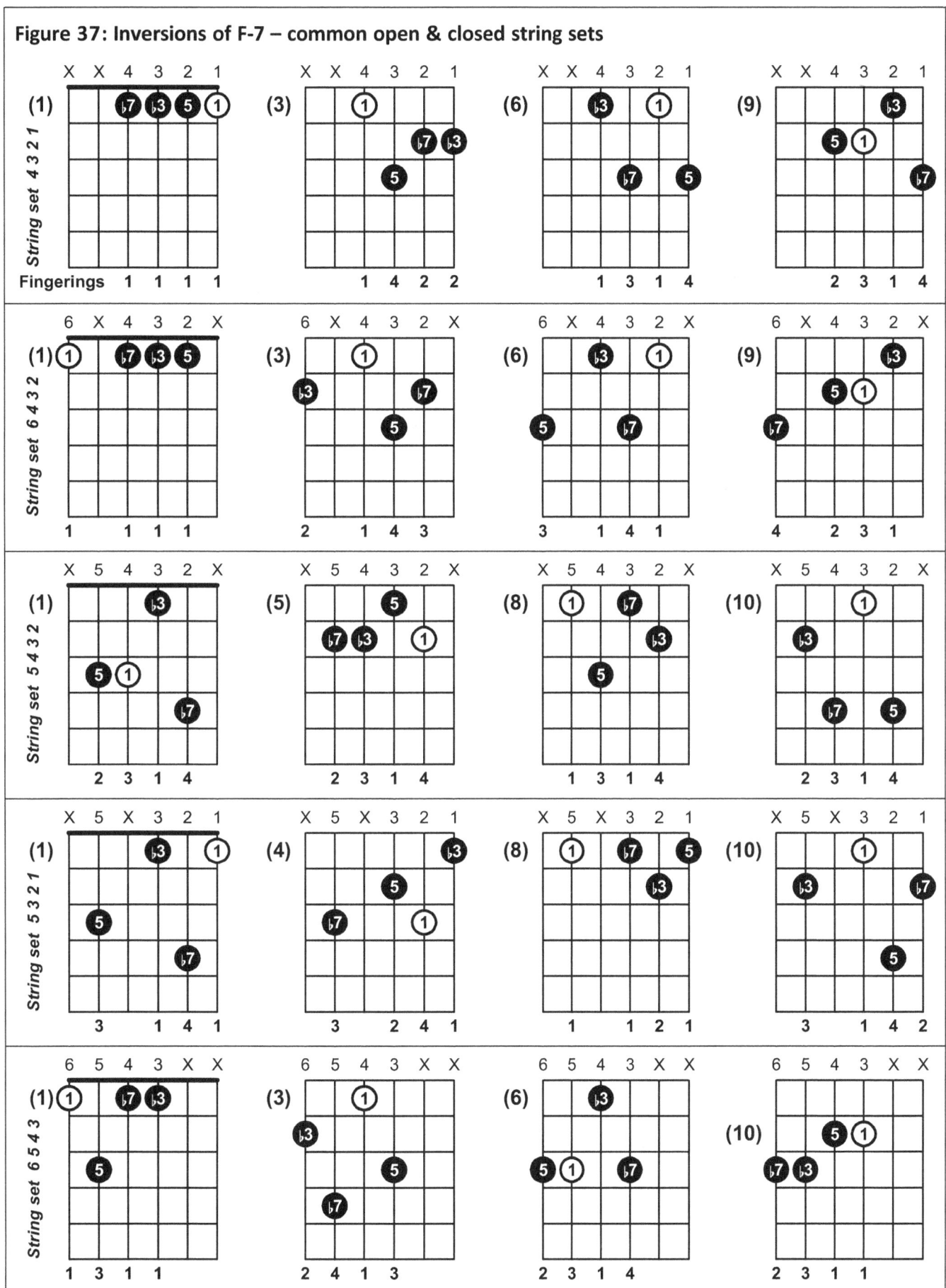

Figure 37: Inversions of F-7 – common open & closed string sets

3- Chords revisited: exploiting tonal distance

Scale tone movement of chords:

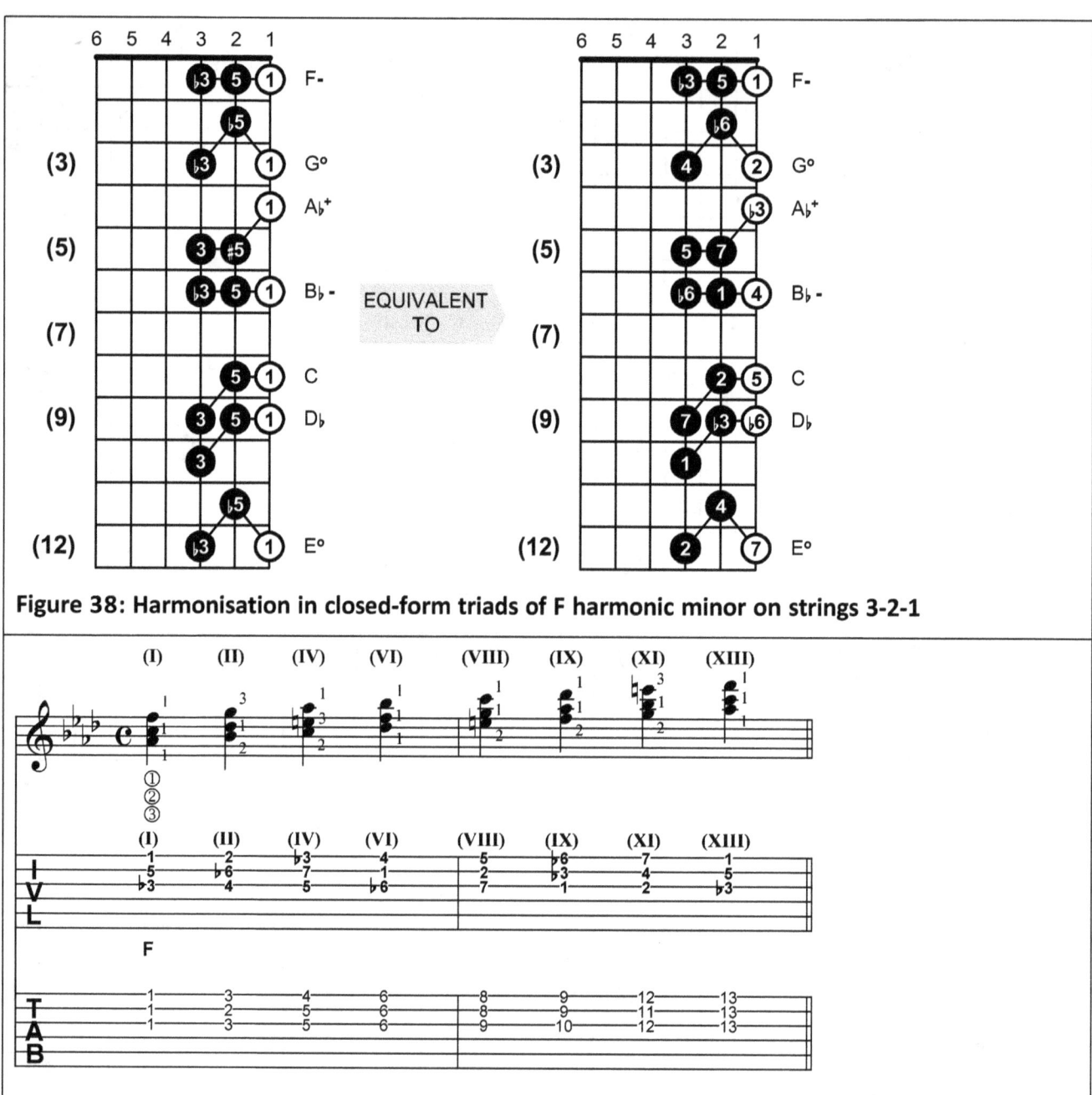

Figure 38: Harmonisation in closed-form triads of F harmonic minor on strings 3-2-1

In the harmonisation example just pictured, the fretboard diagram shows the chords as each having their roots on the 1st string (within F harmonic minor), i.e. F- is 1–5–♭3, G° is 1–♭5–♭3 etc. The "IVL" notation however shows a different interpretation of the same example, where the triads are now made of every other note of F harmonic minor, i.e. F- is 1–5–♭3, G° is 2–♭6–4 etc. – the ability to juggle "non-root" intervals would be quite a boon if you adopt this way of thinking.

Practise harmonising on other string sets. Figure 39 does just that where F melodic minor this time, is harmonised in open-form triads over adjacent string sets. The coverage is expanded across the neck, allowing a range of two octaves. This exercise can be taken further by harmonising in sevenths and so forth.

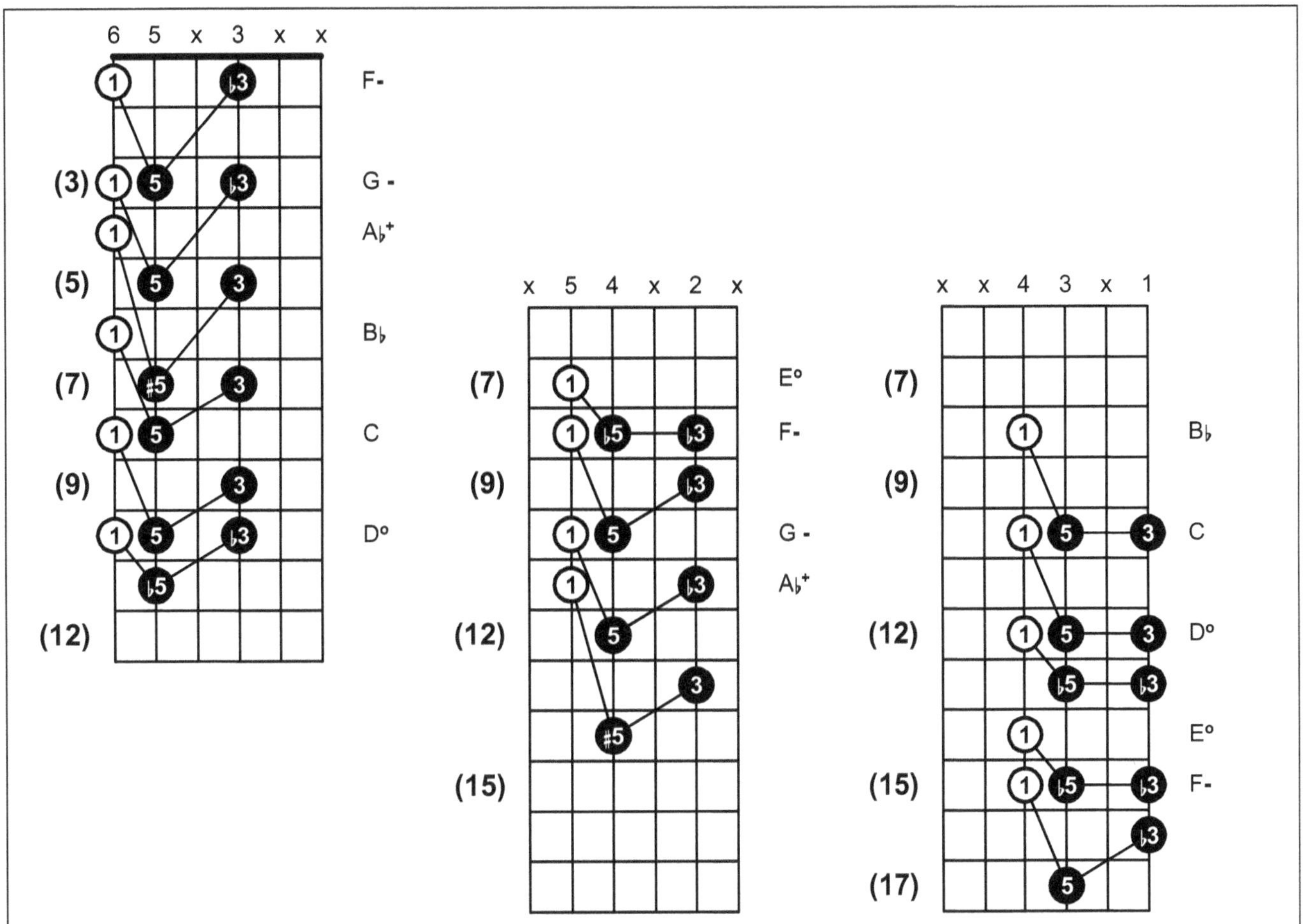

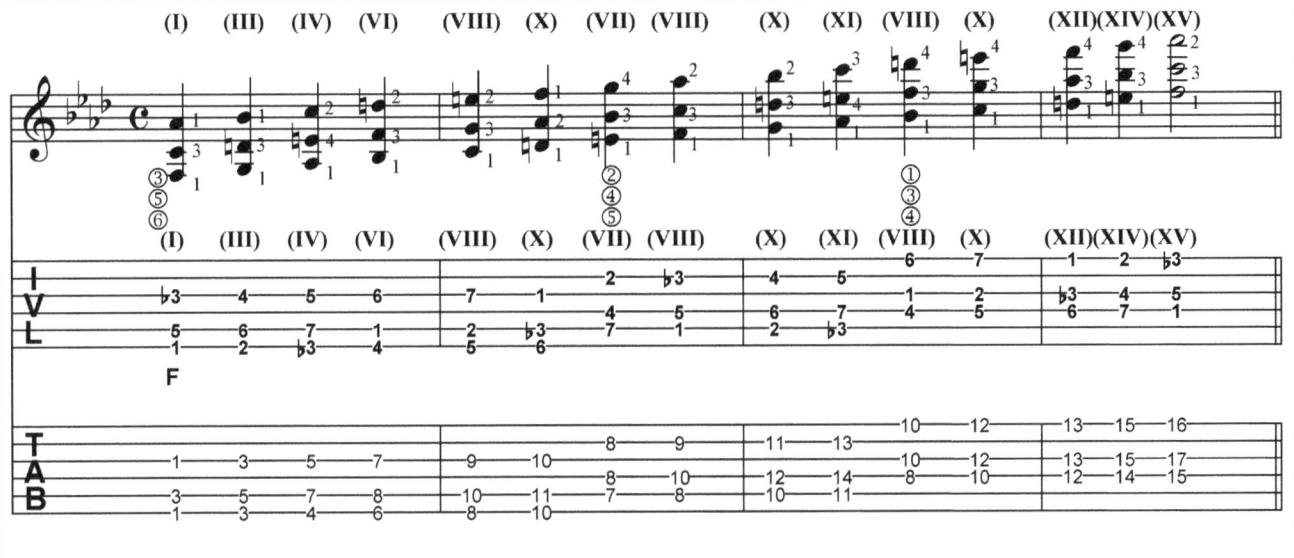

Figure 39: Two-octave harmonisation in open-form triads of F melodic minor on adjacent string sets

3- Chords revisited: exploiting tonal distance

To conclude, the chord progression in Example 12 is a basic I-III-II-I progression in A major. The chords are all triads and exploit fretboard knowledge around the 5th position, playing various voicings of the same chord. A simple manner to create variety by knowing the chord make-up...

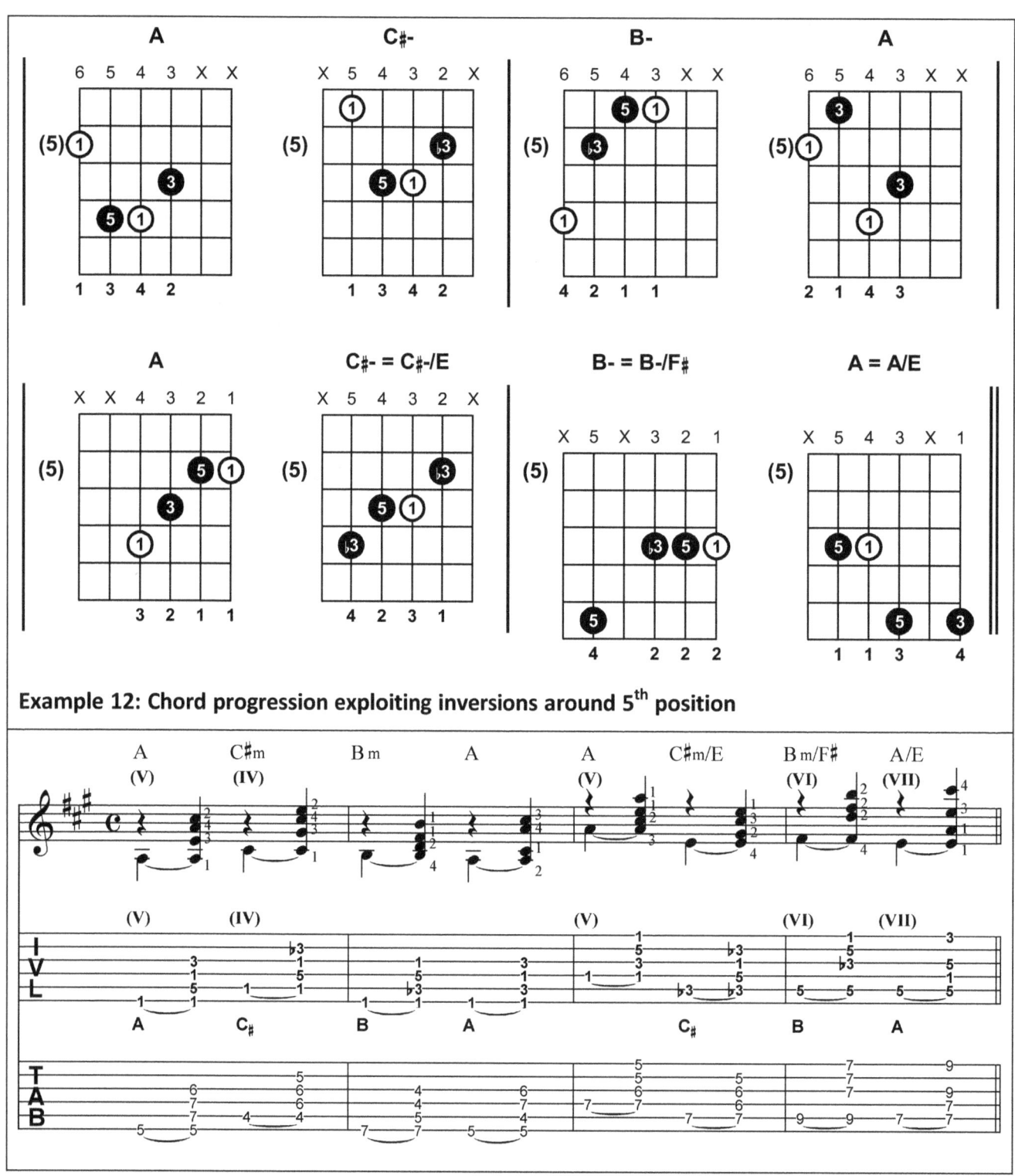

Example 12: Chord progression exploiting inversions around 5th position

Further chordal insight

When confronted with a new chord (or an old one bold enough to learn new tricks!), one ought to analyse resulting chords by permutating the locus of the root, while preserving the shape. To illustrate, we pick examples among triads and 7th chords and watch the transformation as the root is displaced.

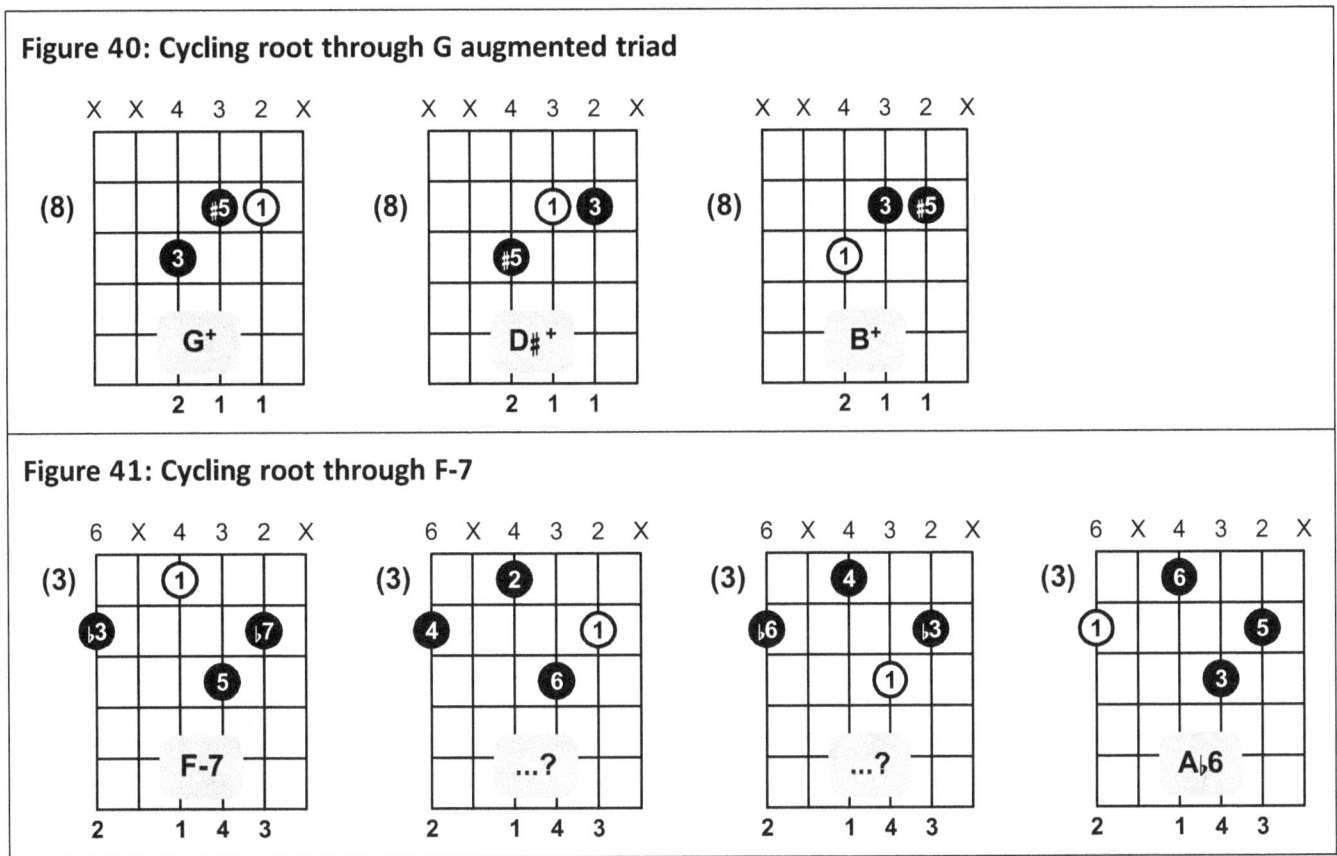

Anecdotally, you may notice that any of the other minor 7th voicings of Figure 37 retains the same chord qualities as those shown in Figure 41, if the root cycles through the chord tones (because the tonal distances within the chord are kept unchanged).

Obviously, in most cases, performing such an operation yields awkward or impractical chord names (left as a question mark in the figures), although occasionally, it can shed valuable light on **chord homonyms**[7] – chords with different names but the same chord tones (e.g. F-7 and A♭6 or G$^+$/D♯$^+$/B$^+$). Nonetheless, the intent is to be able to quickly visualise what becomes of a chord's constituent intervals as the root changes positions with respect to other chord tones. This will dramatically increase your ability and agility in building chord voicings on the fly, knowing what chord tones to keep and which to leave out, as well as recognising unfamiliar chord shapes.

As an exercise, take the F-7 chord of Figure 41 and cycle the other chord tones (♭3, 5, ♭7), as we did with the root.

---

[7] Etymologically, chord *synonym* is the correct appellation because the chords bear different names but the same chord tones (or "meaning"); chord *homonym* literally means chords bearing the same name but a different "meaning". In reality, both terms are used.

3 - Chords revisited: exploiting tonal distance

Manipulating chord tones in such a manner can be stretched further by displacing another chord tone than the root or simply by assigning another degree to a chord tone in a given shape and observing the resulting chord.

Referred to as "non-root" intervals in Chapter 2, the proper thought mechanism here is to strengthen dexterity with relative intervals formed between various degrees of a scale (e.g. between a major 2nd and a perfect 5th degrees, there's a perfect 4th; between a major 6th and a major 3rd degrees, there's a perfect 5th etc.). Avoid referencing everything back to the root – you would be missing the point.

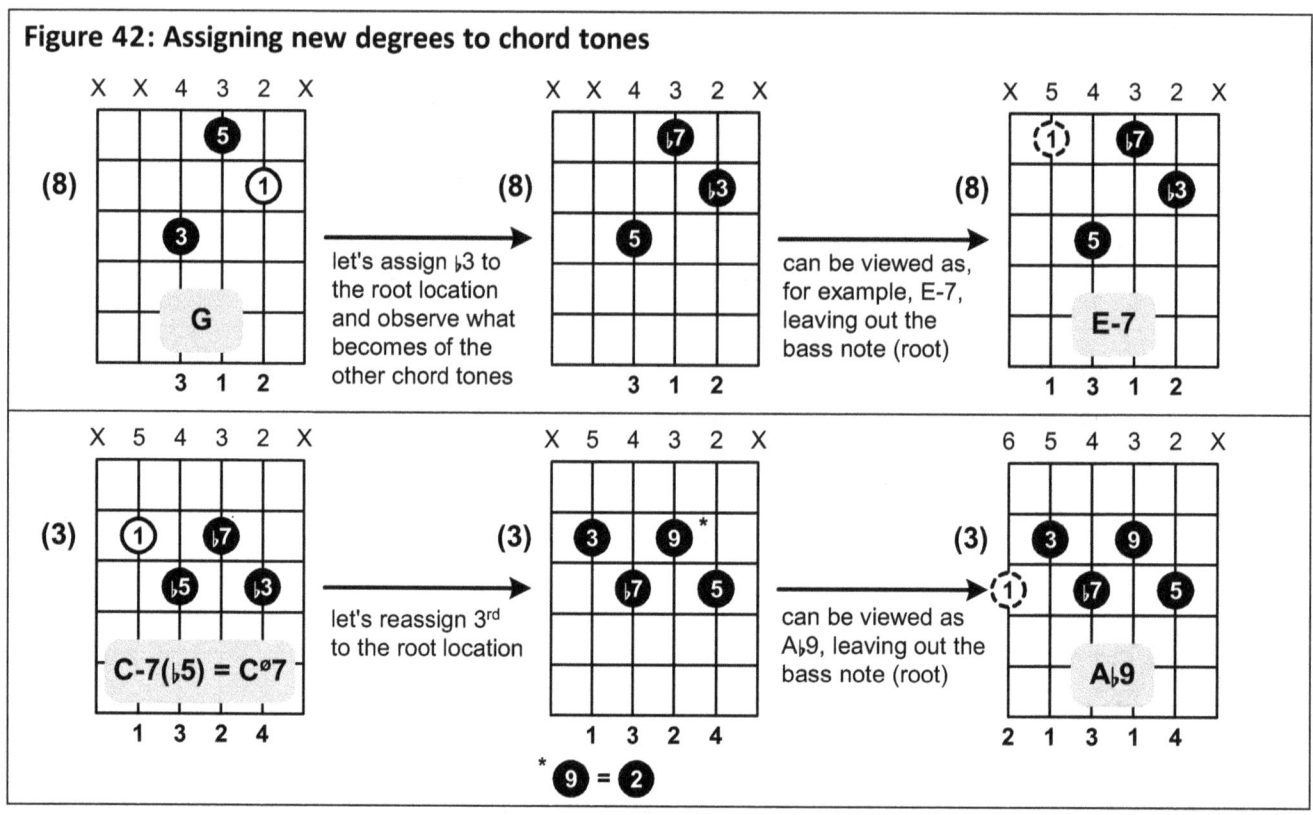

Another manoeuvre would consist in combining the last two: cycling a chord tone amongst existing locations and assigning new degrees to chord tones. Figure 43 demonstrates this idea, while keeping the same chord shape.

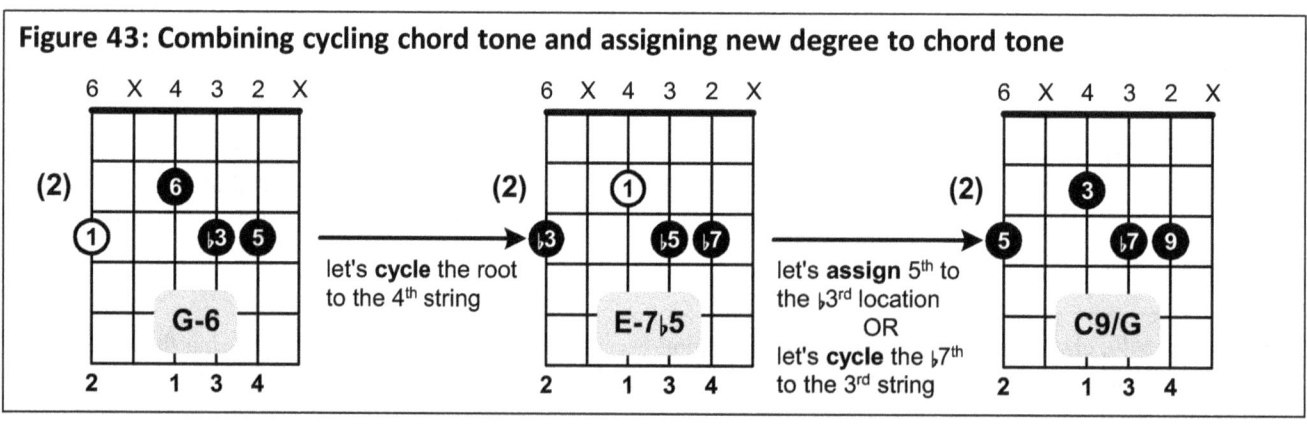

Also, one of the easiest applications of fretboard geometry to chords is the mirroring concept. Several examples can be seen in Figure 35 to Figure 37. Figure 44 shows this idea for a G°7 chord: 2 chords for the price of 1 (albeit a different voicing)!

Another use of fretboard geometry in the context of chords is the 2–3 string shift, which we already discussed in Chapter 2, Figure 29.

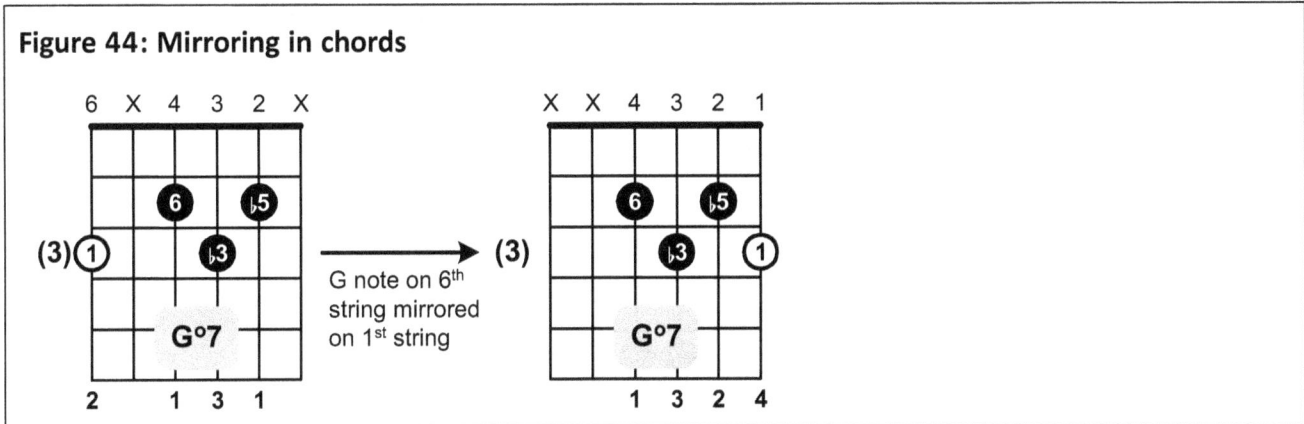

Figure 44: Mirroring in chords

A chord may all of a sudden start looking very much like another, plus or minus a chord tone or two. Beside chord substitution, experienced players will call upon this knowledge to add variety to their comping (e.g. omit chord tones underlined by other instruments, explore new voicings). Intervals give priceless insight into chords.

Visualising chords: chord tones

Guitarists often pick and choose from a number of pre-defined/memorised chord shapes they have learnt. For instance, call a C9 and the following shapes usually come to mind (Figure 45).

As sated earlier, it is very important to attach the intervallic make-up of the chords to those shapes, or to be able to quickly figure them out – something we have been doing all along in this book. Put differently, instead of visualising shapes when C9 is called, we should be able to visualise shapes AND chord tones (Figure 46). The same applies to scales and virtually anything we play, but it is slightly harder with chords since there are several intervals to contend with all at once. Understandably, it would defeat the purpose if you simply mindlessly learn those chord tones by heart; you should be able to determine them instantly (since you have now developed good interval fluency, juggling intervals).

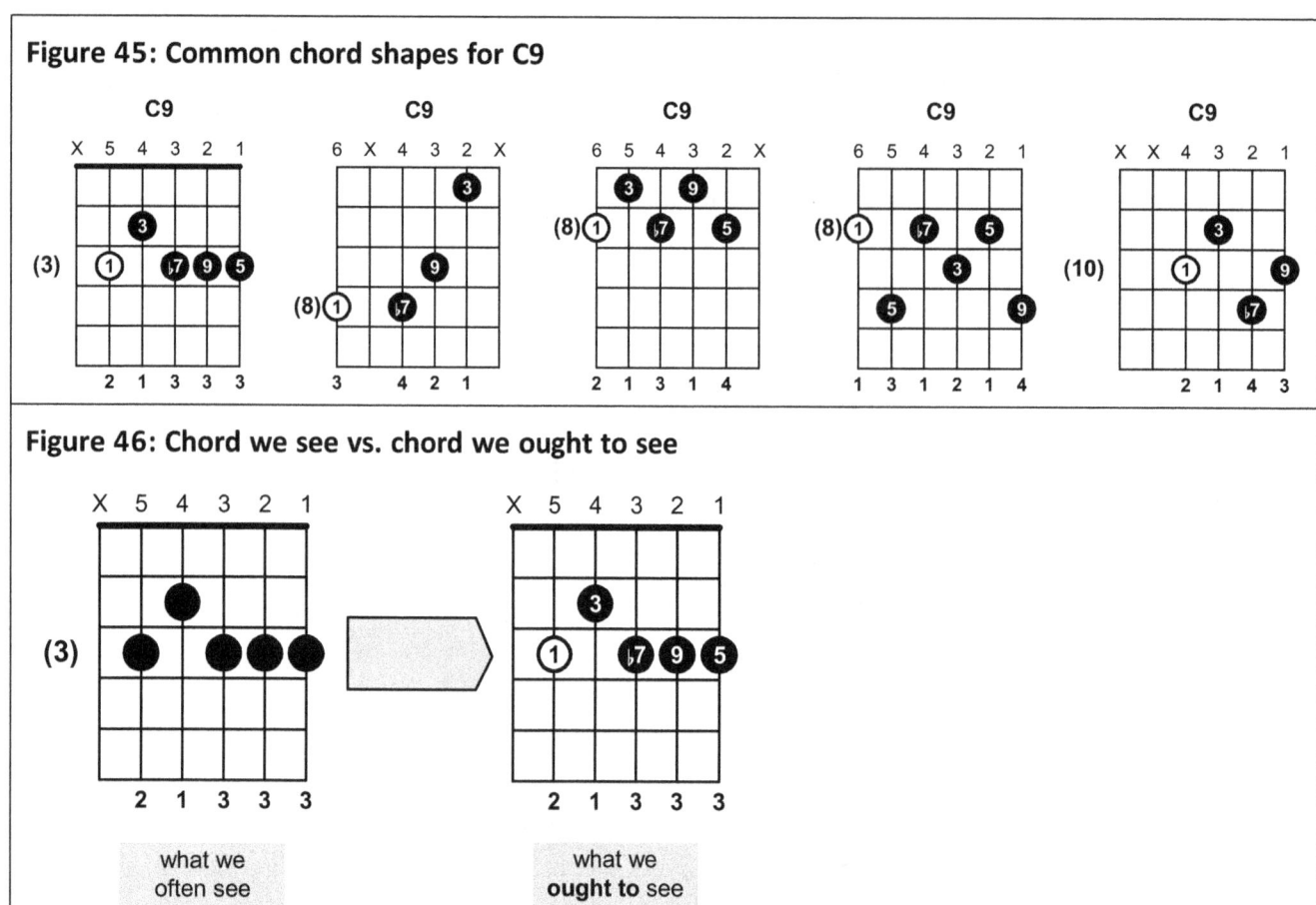

Figure 45: Common chord shapes for C9

Figure 46: Chord we see vs. chord we ought to see

what we often see

what we **ought to** see

There are several compelling reasons for that. First, these are not quite the same chords, despite bearing identical names: some omit the 5th, one doubles the 5th, and the voicings are different (see Figure 45). Then, depending on the musical context, it may be advisable not to play certain notes in these voicings: for example, if a bass player covers the root, then you may elect to leave out the note C when it is in the bottom of the chord, or maybe if the keyboard player is also comping the chords, you may want to highlight part of the chord, the upper three notes only for instance. Or you can decide to imply the chord by only playing a few notes or an interval containing say the ♭7th and the 9th. The bottom line is that there is a lot more you can do with the chords you already know simply by knowing what chord tone is where! And we aren't even mentioning how that knowledge would benefit extending or altering the chord.

But those textbook chords set aside, you should be able to create your own chords. That could be a voicing/fingering that is uncommon but suits a particular musical passage or your own technical ability. But it could also be "new" chords, such as one made of any degrees of a particular scale (also known as scale chords, like 1–2–3–4 of the major scale) or unusual combinations (e.g. an atonal chord made of 1, ♭2, 2, ♭3 degrees; or chords in the context of quartal harmony). A range of new and modern sounds will present itself to you, and not by accident – you "handpicked" every single note in the chord.

4 Interval-based scale and chord derivation: the anchoring principle

Now that we are well-versed in intervals across strings, up and down the strings, let us exploit this concept further. As we derived the triads explained in Chapter 2, we highlighted the 2nd–3rd string intervallic discontinuity, while juggling with 4^{th}s and 5^{th}s elsewhere. That is, we used our knowledge of intervals vertically on the neck. Now, we will expand this horizontally too.

Scale derivation

The anchoring principle:
On a given string, focusing on a given note, it is trivial to see at least a whole step above and below that note, and perhaps farther, on the same string (i.e. expand horizontally). Figure 47 shows the note G, on the 4th string, 5th fret. Assuming we are, for example, in the mode of C Lydian, G is the 5th of that mode. Within reach of G on that very string, there are the 4th, $\sharp 4^{th}$, $\sharp 5^{th}$, and 6th, all within one step (two frets away) from G.

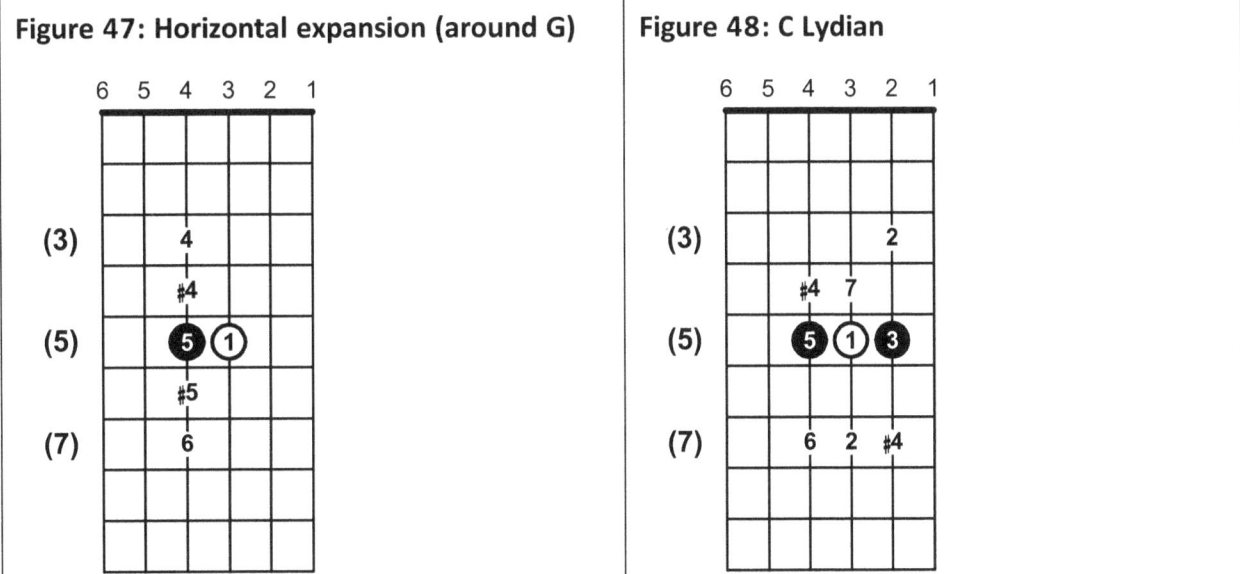

Figure 47: Horizontal expansion (around G)   Figure 48: C Lydian

Now, let's focus on the note C (3rd string, 5th fret). C Lydian is made of the following intervals: 1--2--3--$\sharp$4-5--6--7-8. It should now be a reflex that given C, you would immediately recognise the 5th and 3rd, directly below and above it respectively, on neighbouring strings (Figure 48).
The remaining should fall into place by itself, as it consists of finding all the notes making up C Lydian, around that position.

4- Interval-based scale and chord derivation: the anchoring principle

Around the C on the 3rd string, 5th fret, you have easy access to the 7th and the 2nd. As discussed earlier, the 4th string, 5th fret gives you easy access to the 5th, #4th, and 6th. Last, the 2nd string, 5th fret, puts the 3rd under your fingertips, and the 2nd and even the #4th again are all within reach.

To summarise, given a particular note or **pivot**[8] (the note C here), we could instantly see two additional **anchors**, vertically, within the scale of interest (3rd and 5th here), and use those to expand horizontally.

In a similar fashion we rolled out C Lydian from the 3rd string, 5th fret, we can easily derive other modes/scales and even chords, without referring to scale patterns. For example, if after C Lydian, we move to A Dorian, we locate the closest A requiring minimum or no shift in position (if the goal is to remain within the same position), and picture its anchors (4th and 5th). From those, we can locate the remaining A Dorian notes within reach on adjacent strings with little effort. A Dorian is shown in square boxes in Figure 49, while C Lydian is also pictured. In this particular case, both modes belong to G major (the parent scale) therefore draw from the same note pool. As an exercise, go through the same process with, say, C Aeolian.

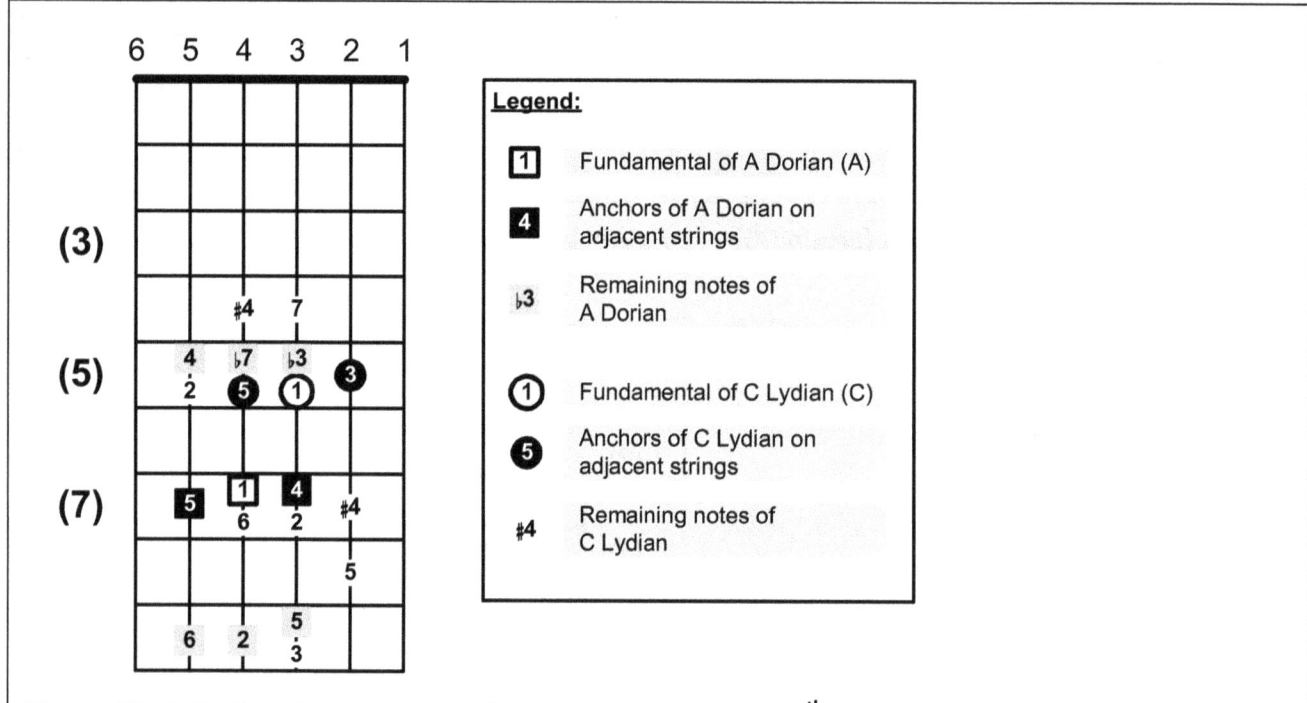

Figure 49: A Dorian shown on top of C Lydian near approx. 5th position

The previous paragraphs warrant a few comments. The fundamental and its anchors are a matter of personal preference. The fundamental serves as a pivot since the anchors and then the scale tones derive from it. Anchors vertically right below and above the pivot – same fret – are convenient because they are merely string intervals (see Chapter 2), but one could pick what best

---

[8] In the text, you may often find the term "anchor" also used to designate the pivot itself, in addition to the pivot's anchors.

4- Interval-based scale and chord derivation: the anchoring principle

suits them. In the previous example, we chose the fundamental of the A Dorian mode, the note A, as the pivot and the 5th and the 4th degrees of that mode as its anchors because they were right below and above the fundamental. The choice of the 5th and the ♭3rd instead for the anchors would have been perfectly legitimate too. In fact, one could choose the 6th of the mode (♮6th with respect to the natural minor), the characteristic note of A Dorian, as the pivot and anchor around that note. Other notes could be selected too. Nevertheless, we feel the fundamental/root is a stronger candidate because the scale/mode is built on it.

Another comment relates to the derivation of the scale on nearby strings (we only showed C Lydian on the 2nd, 3rd, and 4th strings in Figure 48). Naturally, you can expand this principle over all six strings but chances are the line/melody you play will move from one string to a close-by string and you can populate the fretboard "as you go" (there is no need to form a mental picture of C Lydian on the entire fretboard, but only in the area you are playing and are about to play in) – Figure 50.

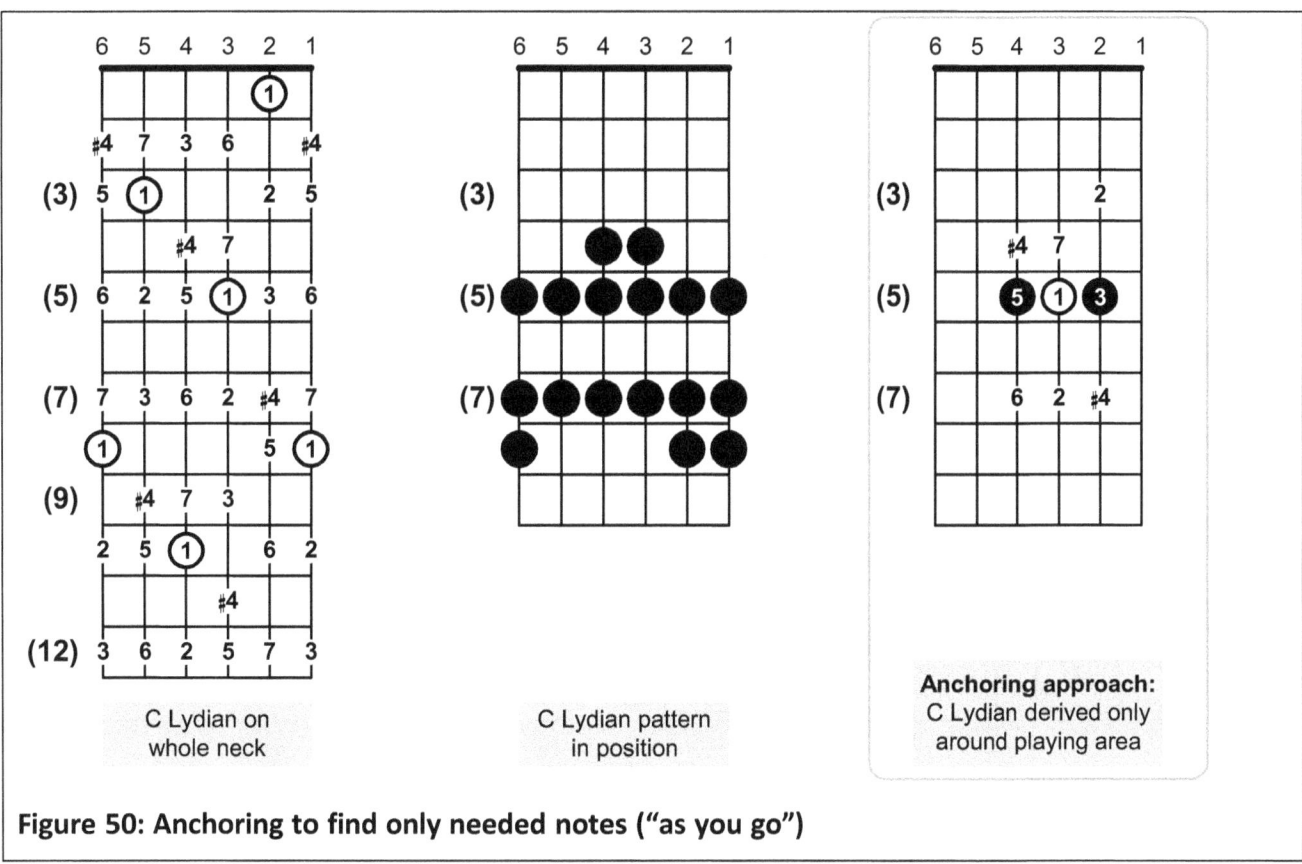

Figure 50: Anchoring to find only needed notes ("as you go")

Example 13 shows this anchoring concept by playing C Lydian over the first bar, visualising the note C (3rd string, 5th fret) and its anchors, before switching gears to D Dorian, picturing the note D (3rd string, 7th fret) and its anchors. All of that is done with the intention of remaining in the 5th position. Evidently, there is no memorised pattern at play here! Only anchors, the knowledge of the scale/mode intervallic construction, and the ability to expand horizontally a few frets around a given note.

4- Interval-based scale and chord derivation: the anchoring principle

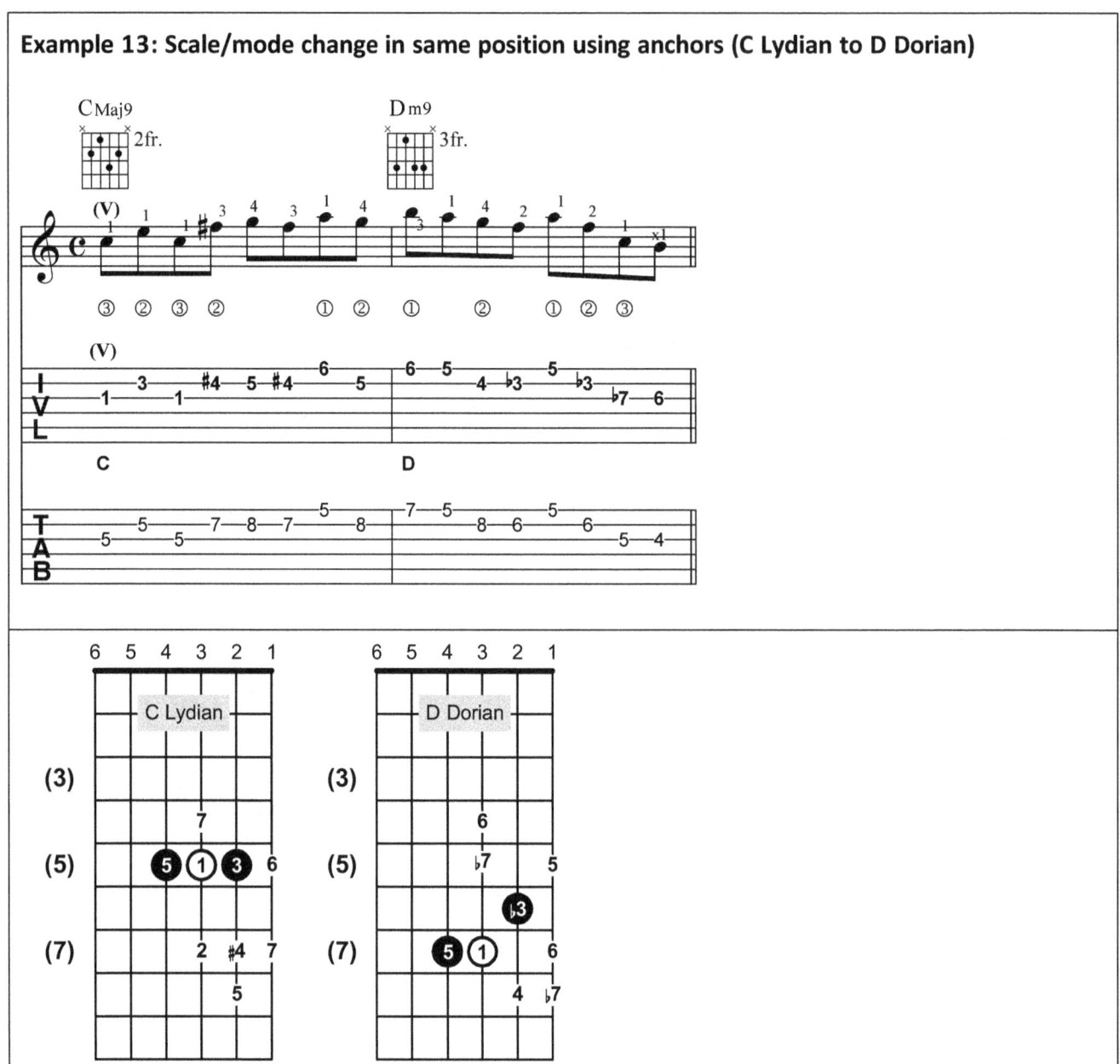

Example 13: Scale/mode change in same position using anchors (C Lydian to D Dorian)

Connecting positions:

In a playing situation however, one does not want to be confined to one position only and longs to have access to the entire fingerboard and its palette of timbres. Helping find an anchor to change positions, *a remarkable property of the guitar in standard tuning is that an instance[9] of the same note always occurs on the fretboard within 3 frets and 3 strings away from any spot on the fingerboard* (Figure 51); Figure 52 shows the same idea in a particular position. Hence, if for starters, the fundamental/root is used as the anchor, there is always another instance nearby to

---

[9] To be exact, two instances of the same note occur on the fretboard within 3 frets and 3 strings away from any spot on the fingerboard.

4- Interval-based scale and chord derivation: the anchoring principle

connect lines or change positions, ensuring never getting lost on the fingerboard (Figure 53 – the note C is on 5th string 3rd fret, 3rd string 5th fret and 1st string 8th fret).

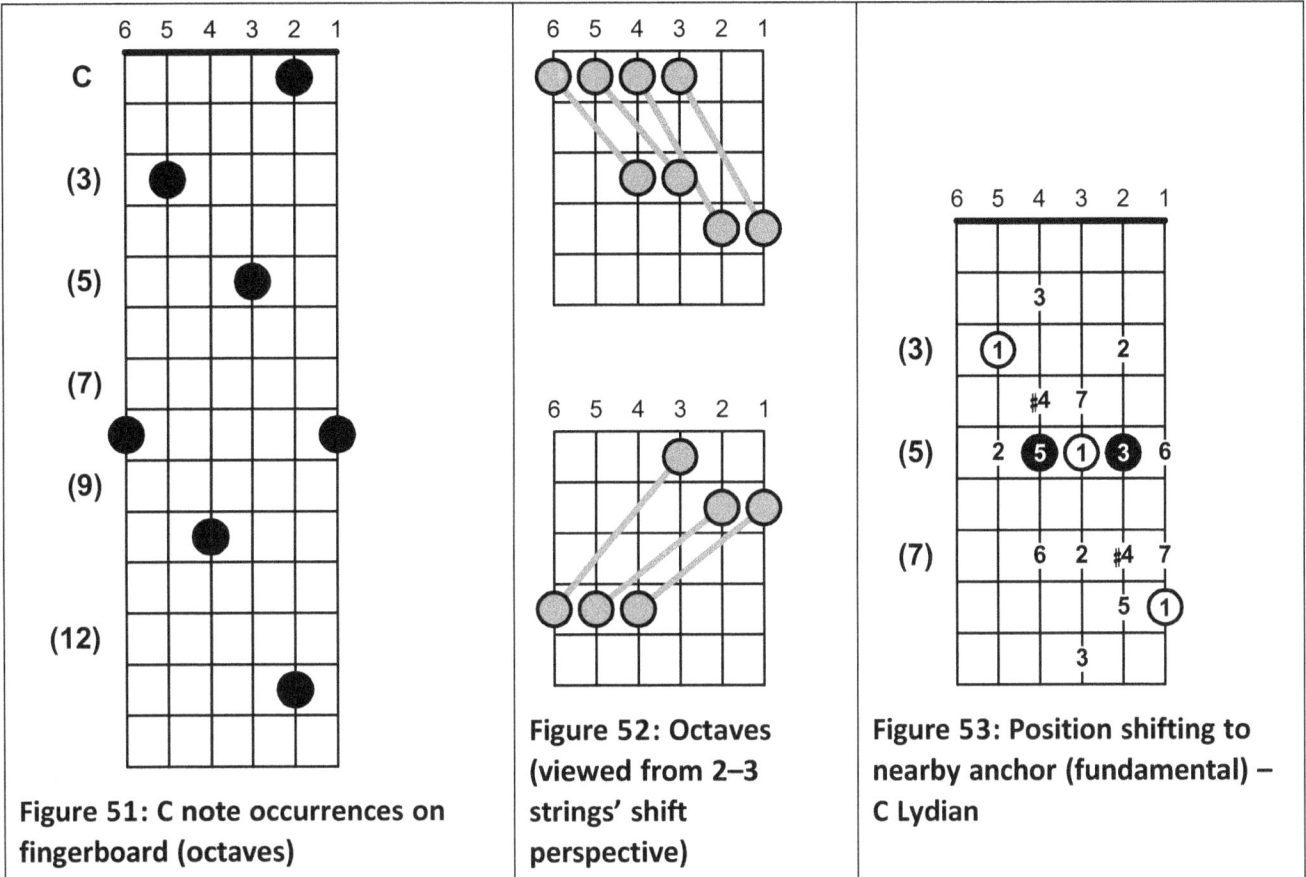

Figure 51: C note occurrences on fingerboard (octaves)

Figure 52: Octaves (viewed from 2–3 strings' shift perspective)

Figure 53: Position shifting to nearby anchor (fundamental) – C Lydian

So far, we have not said much in way of applying an intervallic approach to basic scale exercises. By all means, your standard scale drills can also undergo an intervallic treatment. In Chapter 2, we worked on several diatonic sequence exercises, where it was essential to know which degree of the scale we were on. This is where anchors can come to the rescue.

Example 14 is a straight two-octave C major scale in 5th position, starting with the 4th finger on the 6th string. You may have already learnt this as a pattern elsewhere – but let us build it using intervals and anchors, one note at a time.

In bar 1, we pick C and F (Fundamental and 4th) on strings 6 and 5, as our anchors. These are used to expand horizontally on string 5 and locate D and E (2nd and 3rd).

In bar 2, we change anchors to C on the 3rd string, 5th fret, along with its 5th G below on string 4 and E, its 3rd above, on string 2. Expanding on each string, we obtain the 6th, the 7th and 2nd, and the 4th and 5th.

Finally, in bar 3, we shift to the anchor C on the 1st string, 8th fret. Developing the remainder of the scale on the 1st string gives us the 6th and the 7th. Voilà!

Octave repetition of C was put to use here to locate anchors.

Intervallic Fretboard – Towards improvising on the Guitar

4- Interval-based scale and chord derivation: the anchoring principle

Example 14: Anchoring applied to a scale exercise (C major)

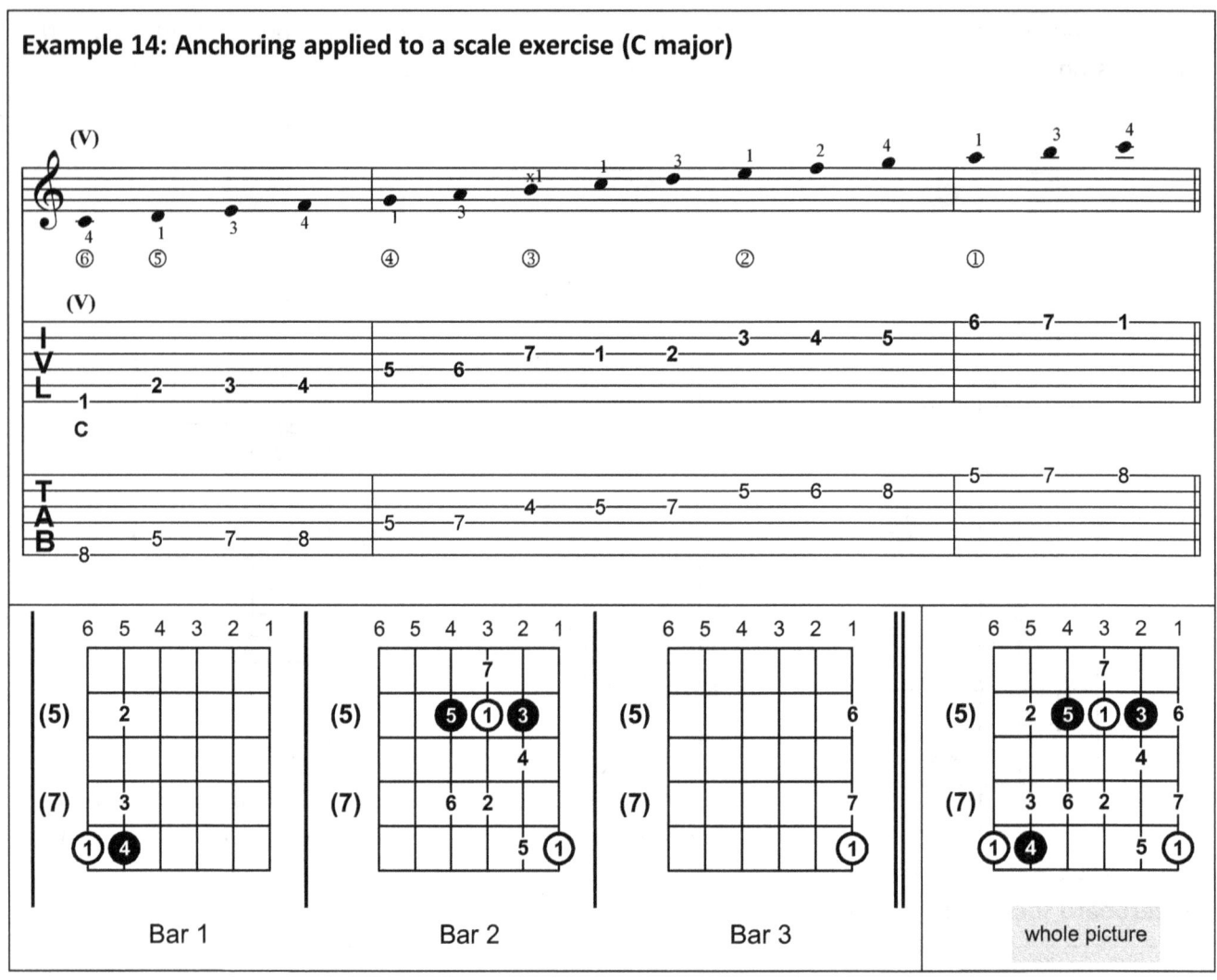

Now, we will develop this idea in a more musical fashion. Example 15 combines anchors and octave repetition in one position across all strings, hitting all notes of the A major scale in that position (that's 18 notes!). It uses the concept of octave displacement, which makes for a lot of string skipping. The result doesn't sound like A major, does it? You have to picture this section of the neck with anchors in its entirety (all at once), because the notes being played jump around quickly. Just like chords, one should see the make-up of the scale being played first, not the pattern.

4- Interval-based scale and chord derivation: the anchoring principle

Example 15: Octave displacement in A major

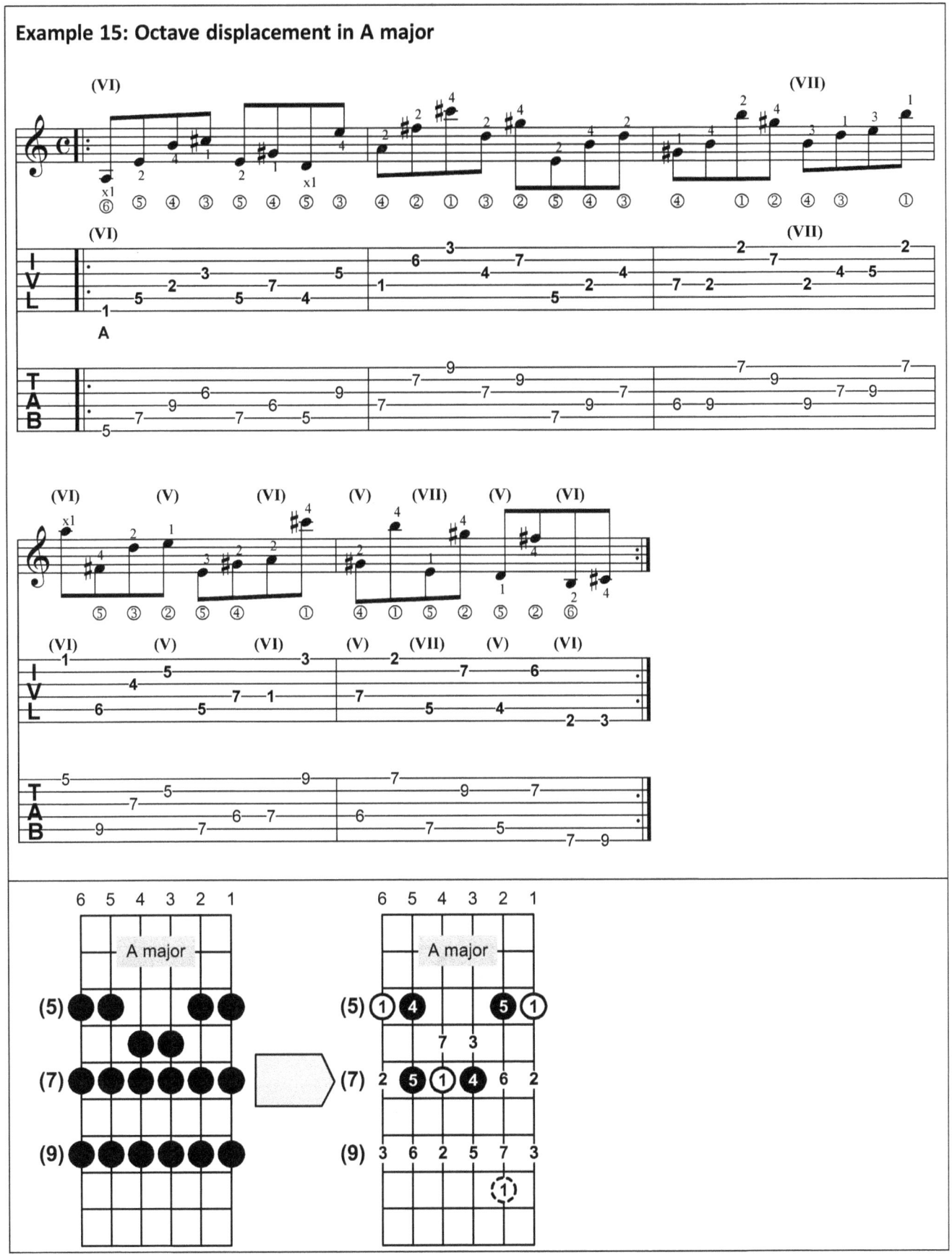

4- Interval-based scale and chord derivation: the anchoring principle

The previous example relied on anchors to cover wide shifts across strings in one position; this next example takes advantage of anchors to move positions across the neck. Example 16 is entirely in C Lydian and starts in the 5th position before moving to 7th position early in bar 2, which ends near the 9th position. Bars 3 and 4 are in 9th position. Along the way, four sets of C notes and their respective anchors have been used, as shown on the fretboard diagrams. As you play the line, you should be able to picture those notes, their anchors, and the notes of C Lydian you need in their vicinity. In bar 1 for instance, we start with the note C on the 3rd string 5th fret and visualise the C Lydian mode around it. Early in bar 2, our vision changes to the note C on the 1st string, 8th fret and the notes of C Lydian around it. At that point, we can afford to "forget" the previous C note: we focus on building a mental image of C Lydian around this new note C on the 8th fret and its anchors. And so on...

With habit, this image will form in the blink of an eye in your mind for a chosen note/anchor.

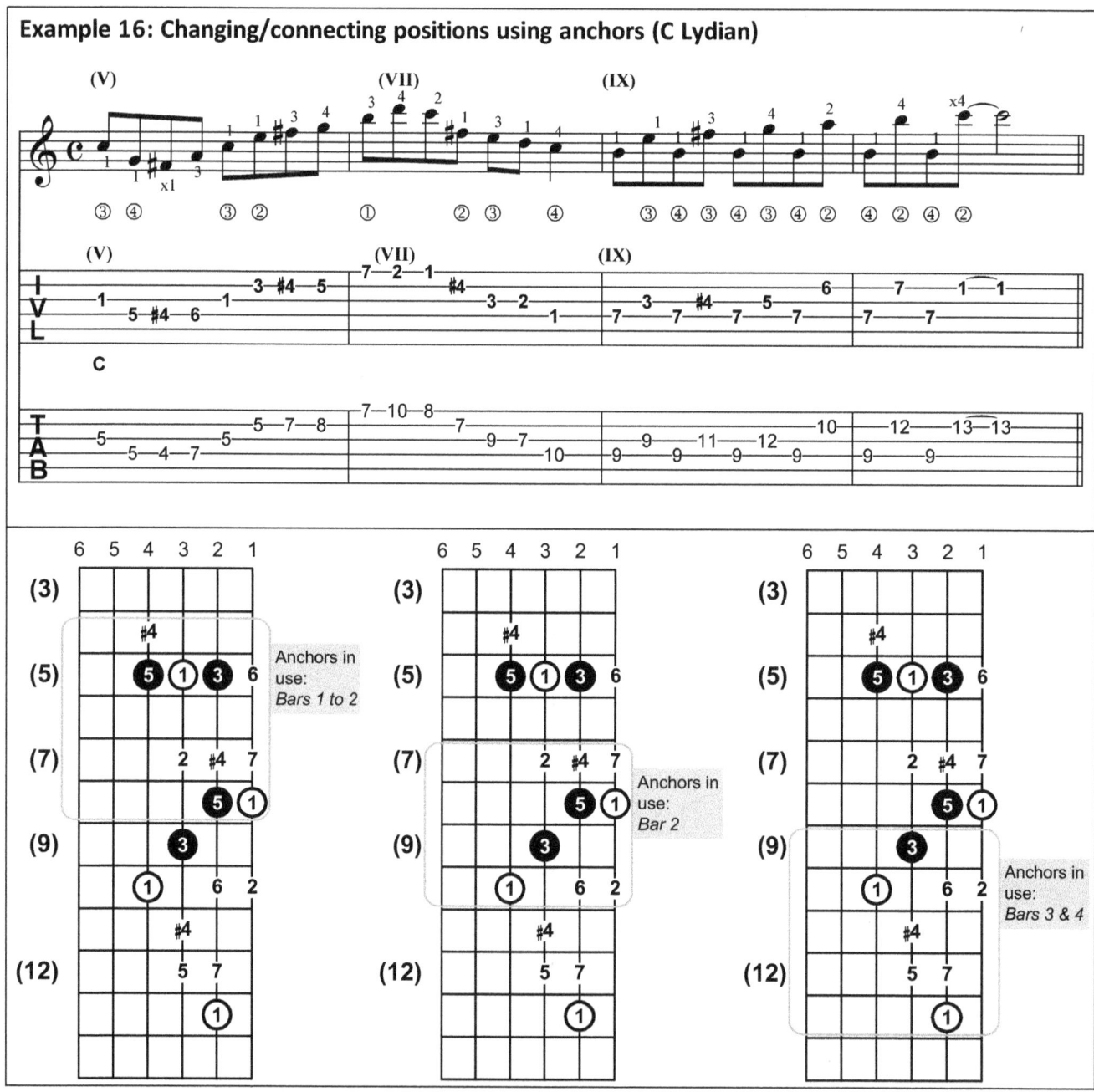

Example 16: Changing/connecting positions using anchors (C Lydian)

Intervallic Fretboard – Towards improvising on the Guitar

4- Interval-based scale and chord derivation: the anchoring principle

Much in the same vein, one can practise changing modes or scales while connecting positions.

<u>Bridge anchors:</u>
Anchors need not be played at all times, they can on occasion serve the sole purpose of landmarks so that you know where you are on the fretboard (harmonically speaking, i.e. is it the 3rd, the ♭6th of the scale or chord etc. you are playing?). An apropos application is that of a single string line or phrase, such as the sequencing of a scale in 3-note motifs, thus quickly shifting positions and needing new anchors to "pave the way".

Example 17 illustrates this point via a sequence in A altered dominant, on the 1st string, moving up the neck in descending and ascending triplets. The first note A (1st string, 5th fret) is obviously an anchor but unlike other examples studied so far, the next anchor, A again, only occurs at the 17th fret, too far away to safely connect the line from one anchor to the next – in other words, chances are one might get lost in-between. The solution, once more, is to take advantage of the fingerboard's layout. There may not be another note A between the 5th and 17th position on the 1st string, but there certainly is one[10] on the adjacent 2nd string, on the 10th fret. And that note on the 2nd string, although not played, can be leveraged to situate ourselves when we are too far from the first note A (5th fret), and not quite near enough to the second note A (17th fret). This **bridge anchor** or *auxiliary anchor* gives us the ♭5 of A altered dominant as an anchor to latch onto, right above it on the 1st string, 11th fret (one could have also opted for the 3rd as an anchor). Knowing the make-up of A altered dominant (1-♭2--♯2-3--♭5--♯5--♭7--8), we can then safely play the line, connecting the first note A (5th fret) to the second note A (17th fret) thanks to the intermediary anchors (A on the 2nd string 10th fret and its resulting anchor ♭5 on the 1st string). The knowledge of the notes of A altered dominant (A-B♭-C-D♭-E♭-F-G), although useful, is of lesser importance than its intervallic make-up with respect to the fundamental.

Therefore, anchors – whether played or not – buy us fingerboard visibility in their proximity, on adjacent strings (maybe even farther) and at least a couple of frets above and below them, on a given string. That is after all a sizeable area.

---

[10] We could have also used a "mirror" anchor (above the 1st string, one can picture the mirrored 5th string with the note A occurring on the 12th fret, which gives us the ♭5th right below it on the 1st string, 11th fret. See Chapter 2, Figure 17). But that is a far-fetched idea!

4- Interval-based scale and chord derivation: the anchoring principle

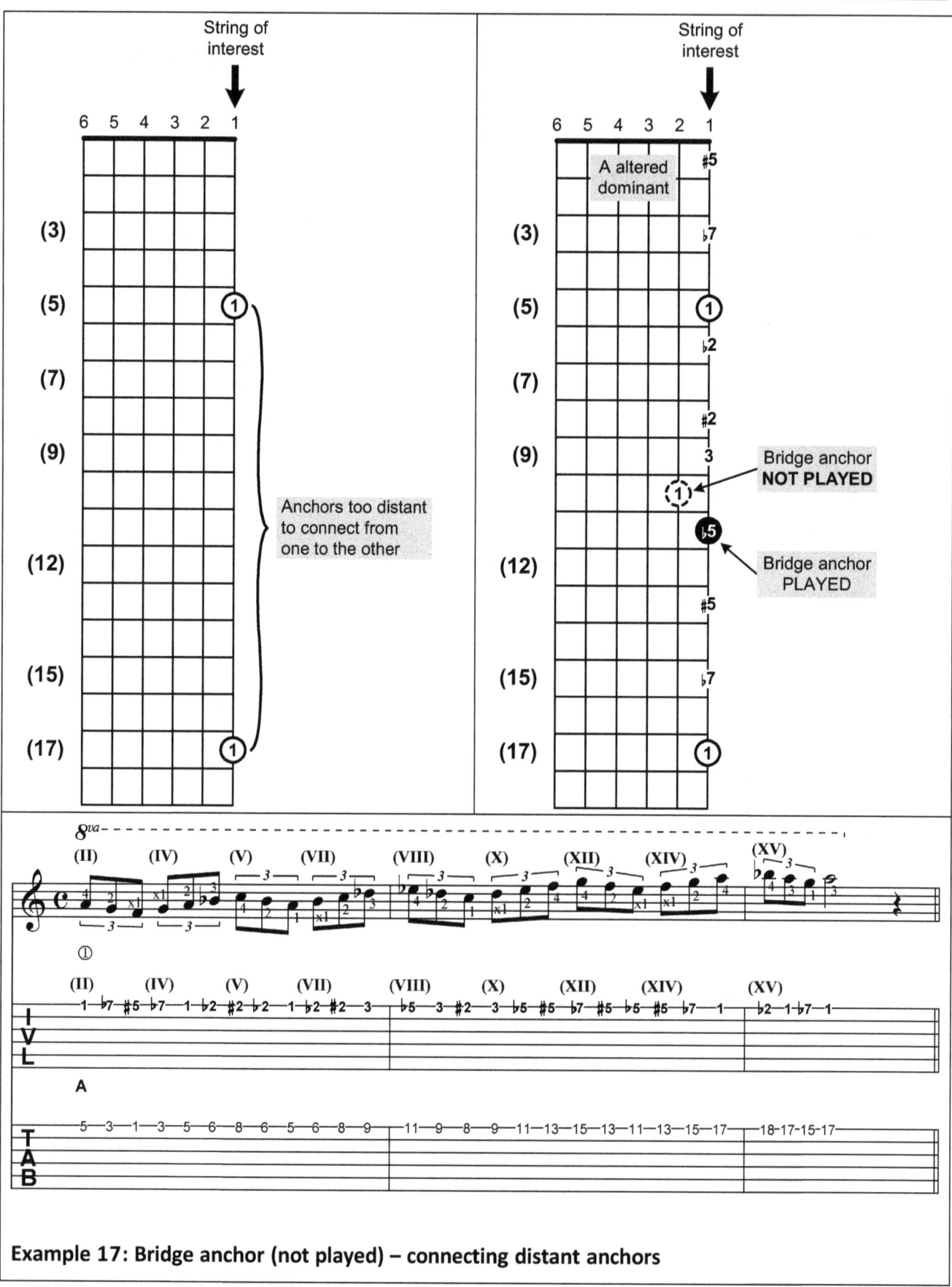

Example 17: Bridge anchor (not played) – connecting distant anchors

4- Interval-based scale and chord derivation: the anchoring principle

Example 18 combines the anchoring concepts explained in this section in a blues example/lick. The line is in B blues (with passing notes C#/2nd in bar 1 and A#/7th in bar 2), and shifts keys to E pentatonic minor in bar 3 (again with a passing note F#/3rd). Observe the use of bridge anchors, which are called upon simply to aid in note placement, but are not played.

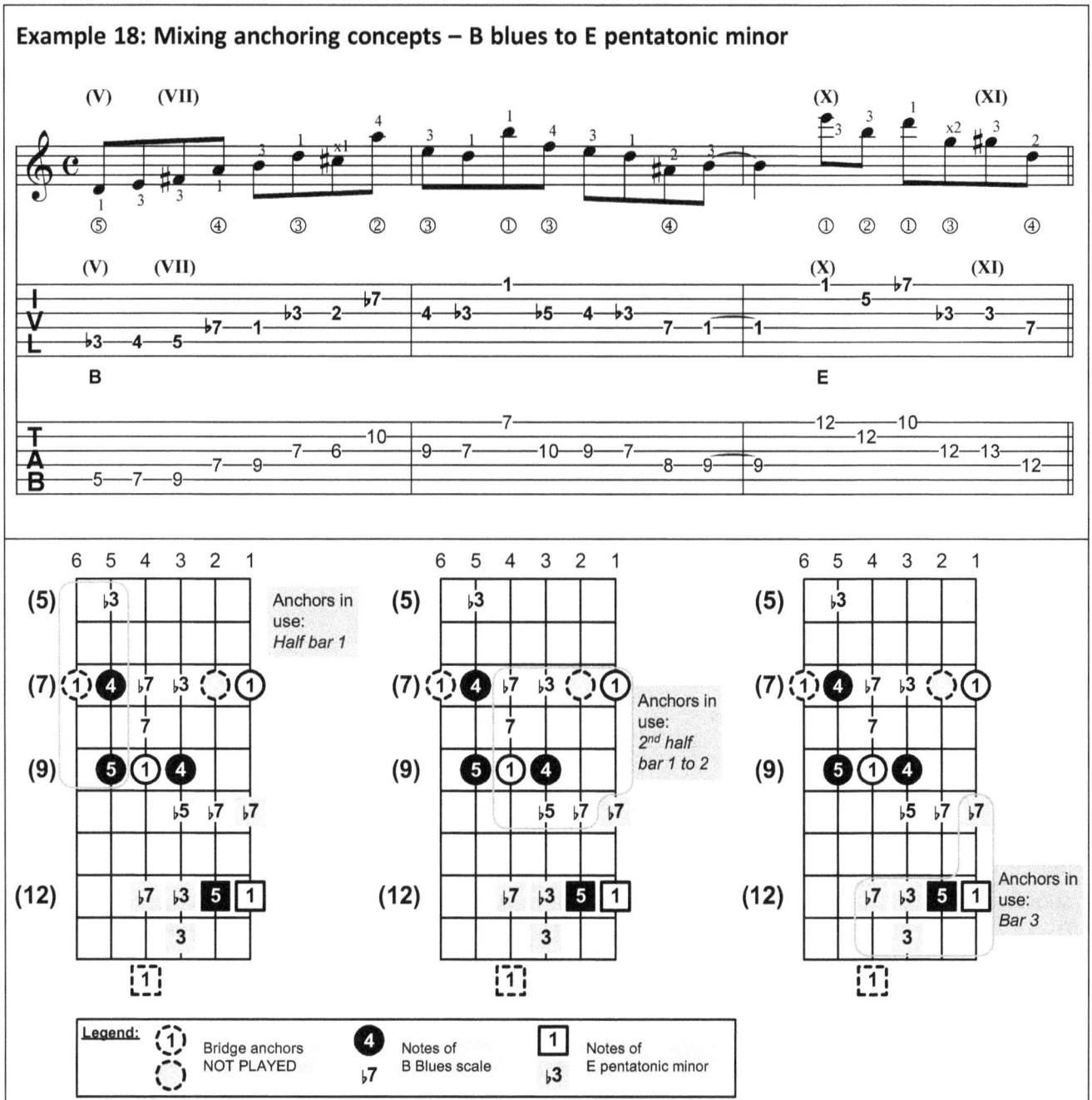

4- Interval-based scale and chord derivation: the anchoring principle

Chord/arpeggio derivation

As easily as a scale was derived, a chord can be derived. Let's stay in C Lydian and derive a particularly Lydian chord: Cmaj7(#11) – Figure 54 – soloing with chord tones got a lot easier all of a sudden! The form it takes is more prone to chord tone soloing rather than holding a chord form or playing arpeggios.

Figure 55 shows a D11 arpeggio (incidentally also part of C Lydian), spanning over two positions (approx. 5th and 7th positions), across all strings. Two sets of anchors were used (5/1/4 near 5th position and 1/3 in 7th position). 5/1/3 would have been another good choice of anchors near the 5th position. Note that speaking of the #11th and 11th would be more proper here in the context of chords/arpeggios.

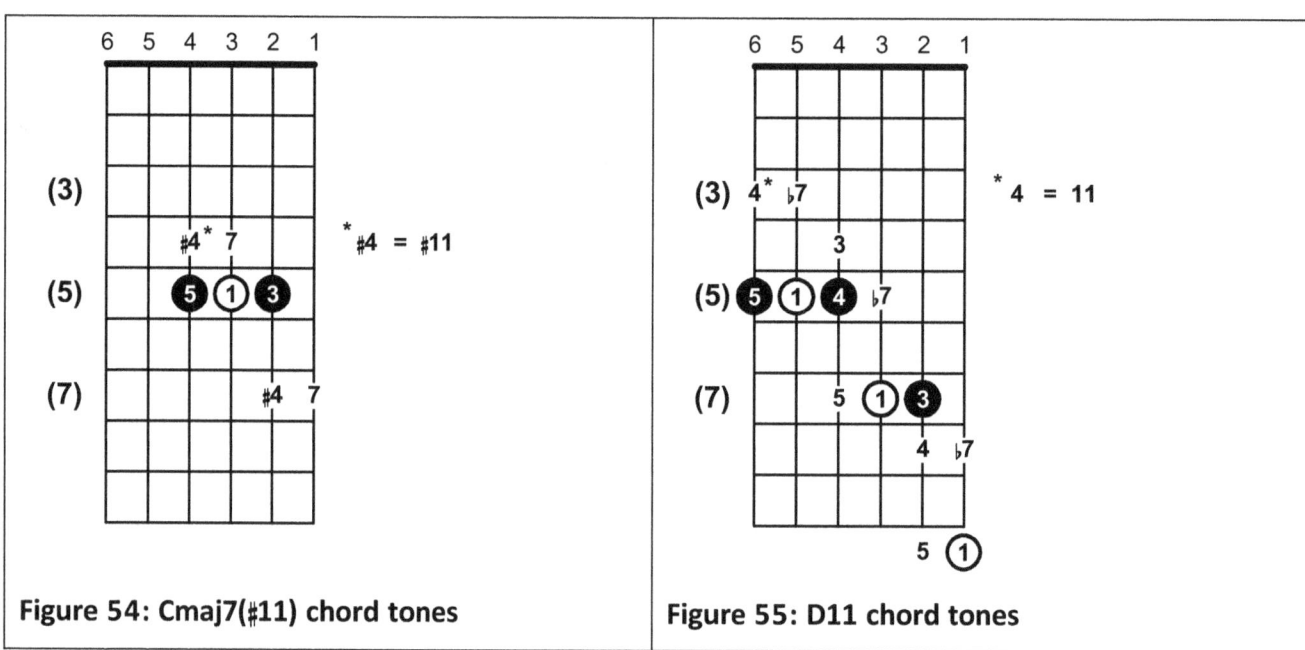

Figure 54: Cmaj7(#11) chord tones   Figure 55: D11 chord tones

Example 19 illustrates the building of arpeggios (or broken chords) using the anchoring principle. The backdrop is a "Condensed Blues": a I-V-IV-I blues type progression in A over only four bars, hence the name. To add to its appeal, the progression resorts to extended and altered dominant chords instead of simple dominant 7th chords. Some stepwise voice leading also occurs within those chord changes. But the objective is the arpeggios! They articulate the extended/altered chords and for the most part, make the transitions from one chord to the next very smoothly via a half or a whole step. At times, the arpeggios do exhibit a couple of large intervallic jumps to increase melodic interest. It is paramount to note that the arpeggios do not go back to the root of the chord when there is a chord change, they simply move on to whatever note that is close-by (on same or adjacent string), but part of the next chord in the progression – this ensures the arpeggios connect seamlessly to one another. And there are no position changes; the line is played entirely in the 5th position. The "IVL" notation clearly shows what is happening. While playing through the example, try to picture the chord's fundamental and its anchors, as we did in the previous examples – the chord tones should then fall into place by themselves on the fretboard.

4- Interval-based scale and chord derivation: the anchoring principle

Although the rhythmic pattern is irrelevant for the purpose of this exercise, a shuffle feel may be more pertinent than straight quarter notes.

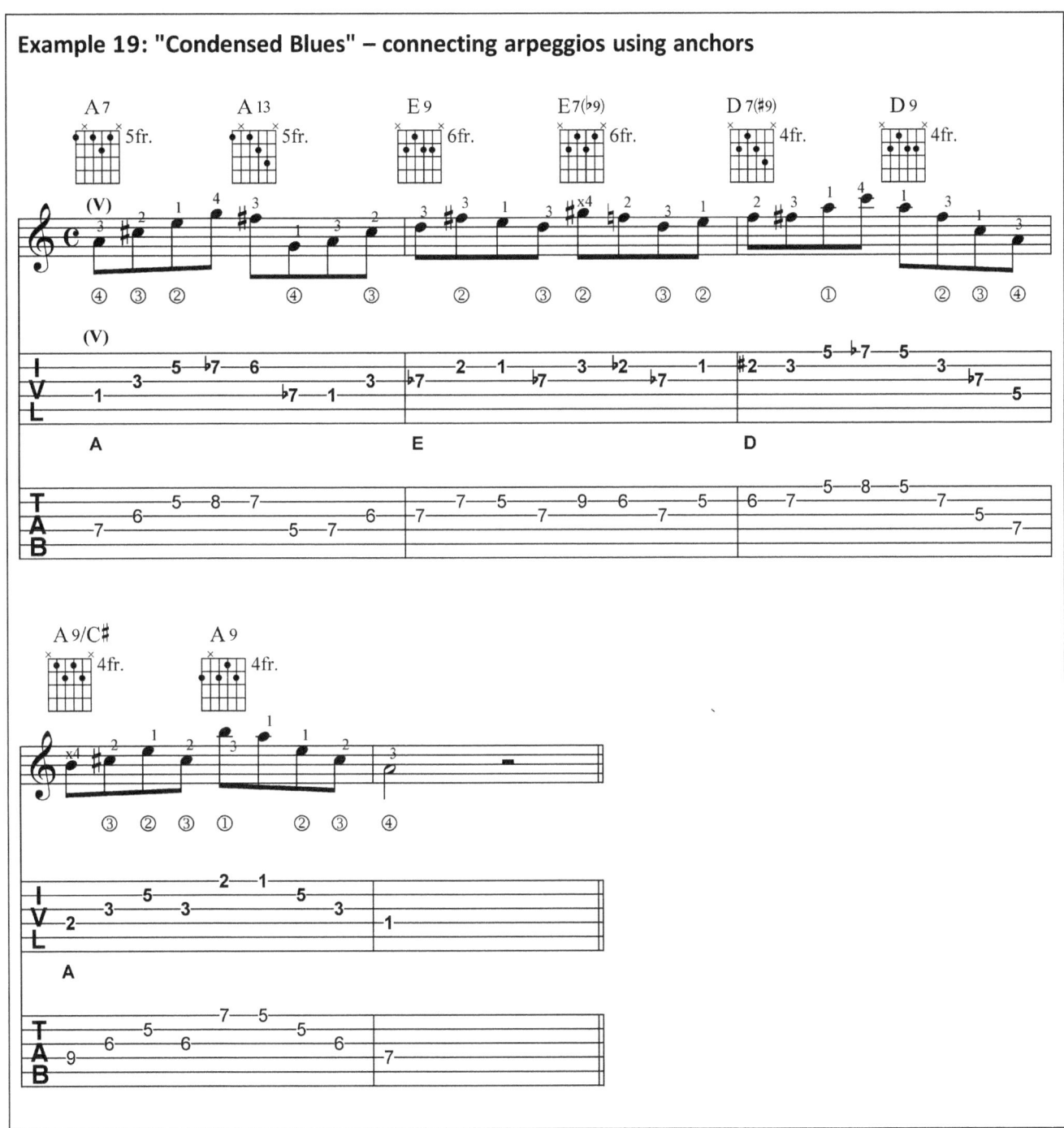

Example 19: "Condensed Blues" – connecting arpeggios using anchors

The anchoring principle can be effectively applied when playing clusters of notes, such as intervals or triads. Example 20 is reminiscent of the double-stop exercises in Chapter 2...but let us examine how anchors can aid in this respect.

The example is in the key of A major, playing a double-stop sliding into another and back to the original double-stop. The picture being formed on the fingerboard need only be that of the original

Intervallic Fretboard – Towards improvising on the Guitar

4- Interval-based scale and chord derivation: the anchoring principle

double-stop and the double-stop it is sliding into, along with anchors. Nothing else. Other notes in the scale of A major are totally ignored until played.

The first bar is an interval formed by the fundamental and the 5th, sliding into an interval formed respectively by the 2nd and the 6th of the scale, and back. No other note needs to be visualised on the fingerboard at this stage. The fundamental and 5th serve as anchors to this cell. The next bar is an interval formed by 5th and 3rd, sliding into the 6th and 4th and back. The 5th and 3rd serve as anchors to this cell. The following cell is an interval formed by the 3rd and the fundamental of the scale, sliding into the 4th and 2nd and back (3rd and fundamental serve as anchors). The exercise ends with an A major triad (5–1–3).

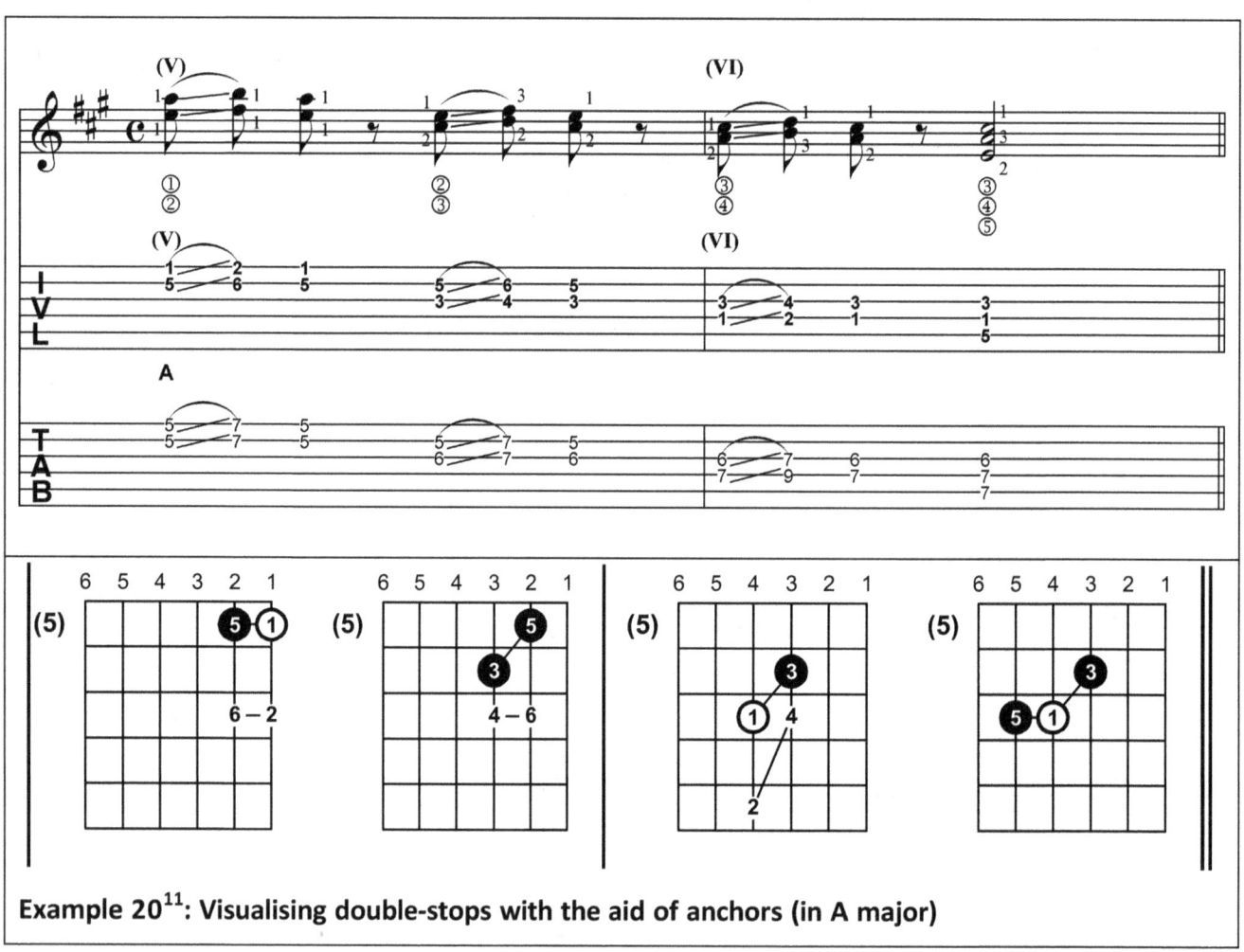

Example 20[11]: Visualising double-stops with the aid of anchors (in A major)

---

[11] Position playing applies ambiguously or freely in an interval or chordal context. In the first bar, the index finger slides from 5th to 7th position and back to 5th position, but the position is marked as 5th position all along. This is because the thumb stays put behind the neck (no movement of the thumb) while the index finger slides. Alternatively, a position shift from 5th to 7th and back to 5th could have been marked too and is also legitimate.

4- Interval-based scale and chord derivation: the anchoring principle

When the single line meets the harmony: chord-melody

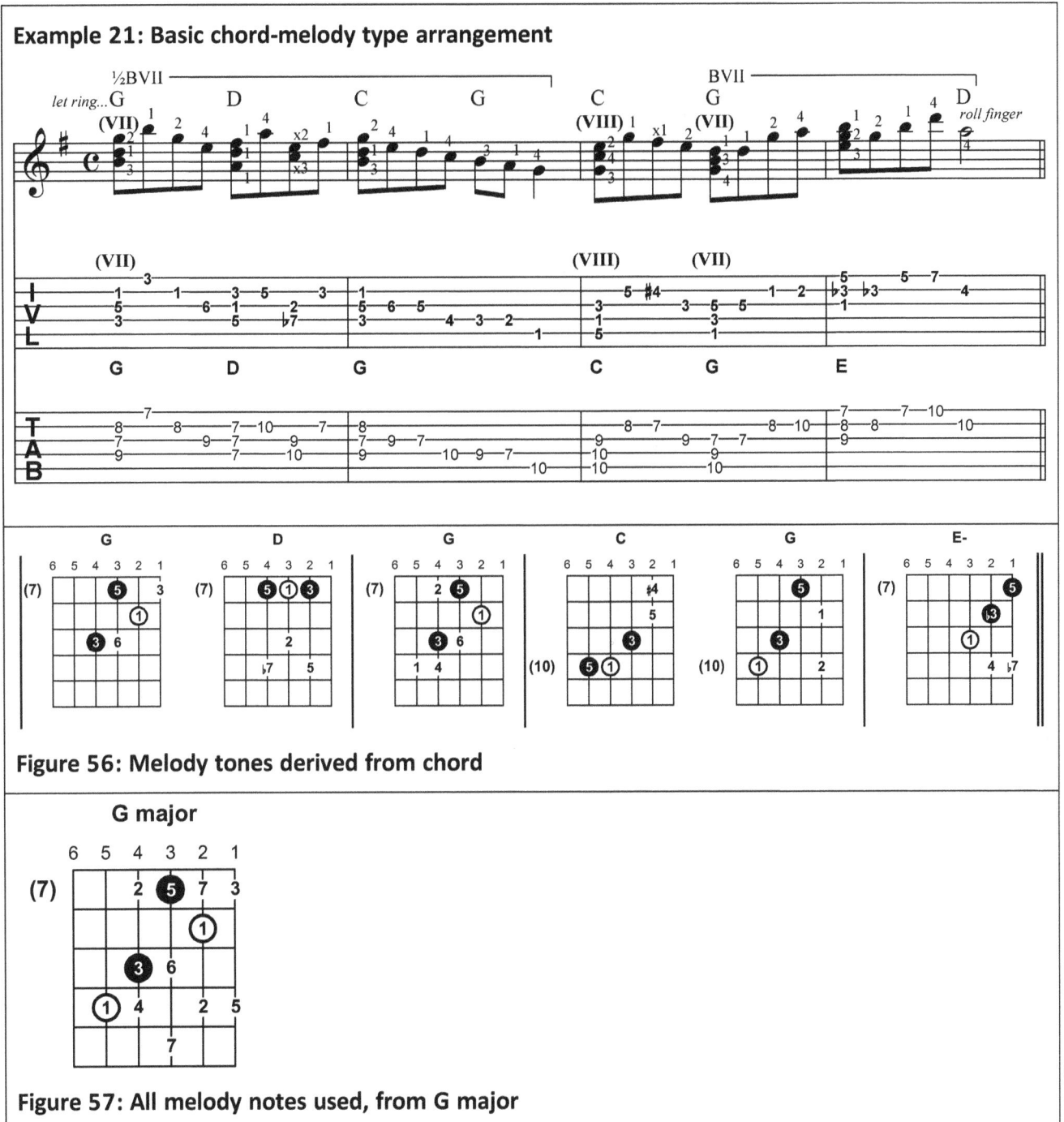

Figure 56: Melody tones derived from chord

Figure 57: All melody notes used, from G major

Combining a chord position with scale tones in its vicinity, a chord-melody type phrase can be created, or chords can be embellished by adding scale tones. Example 21 is such an arrangement of a short excerpt inspired by a familiar Irish/American fiddle tune titled "Blackberry Blossom". The piece is in the key of G but for this exercise, instead of interpreting all the melody as belonging to the key of G, we will view the single lines from the standpoint of each chord they originate from. Most of the lines can be played while holding down the chord (most are barred) and reaching for the melody notes with spare fingers. Once more, knowledge of the chord tones' location is essential in building the scale tones around the chord. Underneath the score, charts show the chord tones for each chord and the scale/mode tones derived from it – those notes should eventually pop up in front of you when playing.

The chords and melody lines all belonging to the key of G major, one could have chosen to view all chords and melody notes based on G major, rather than individual chords. Every single note played in the four measures is shown in Figure 57; all notes are extracted from the G major scale and shown with G as the fundamental (or pivot) and its anchors B and D.

Anchors are ad hoc landmarks: they will help map out your way on the fretboard. Eventually, with practise once more (nothing has yet bettered practise!), you will instantly start seeing 3^{rd}s, 6^{th}s, 2^{nd}s etc. – all the scale tones – around the fundamental/root you choose, the anchors will become notes among others.

To summarise the framework for applying interval thinking in a practical manner, remember the following points:

Synopsis:

1. Decide what to play or draw from (scale, mode, chord tones etc.).
2. Locate the root of the line to play, within the position chosen to play in. (this location may depend on the previous playing position)
3. Visualise immediate anchors (typically the 3rd and the 5th or the 4th on adjacent strings to the root will jump out). With time, notes will light up[12] on more strings (e.g. 2nd and 7th two strings away might be candidates).
4. Expand horizontally. This might be more applicable if you opted for a line based on scales rather than chord tones. Depending on how comfortable you are with patterns, those may start appearing at this point, further expanding the chartered territory.
5. As the line comes to an end and/or there is a change in the progression, think of what you want to play next, and locate possible anchors.
6. Go back to step 1.

---

[12] One-of-a-kind guitarist Allan Holdsworth once said that "when I look at the neck, the notes just light up where those scales would be". This is the goal.
From interview of Allan Holdsworth by Steve Adelson in Twentieth Century Guitar Magazine, Sep. 2000.

5 "Lessons learnt!"

Let us pause for a moment and review the concepts we have covered so far, what we ought to have learnt and internalised, and how it should be driving our thought process...before moving forward.

Points to remember

Thinking and visualising intervals may be new to you, and like all things new and fresh, require getting accustomed to.

1- First, you should now be intimately familiar with intervals separating adjacent strings (up and down) and becoming comfortable with intervals separating non-adjacent strings.

2- Next, you must be able to instantly play any triad (major, minor, diminished, augmented, suspended etc.) on three adjacent string sets, without having to resort to shapes, but by stacking intervals, and you should be able to identify the harmonic function of each note (e.g. know that sus4 chord is 1–4–5). Simply put, mastery of the interval and its 3-note counterpart, the triad, is mandatory. Anchoring to build scales and chords or stacking intervals all rely on your ability to see notes in 2 or 3-note clusters. It is highly recommended that you recognise (more so than memorise) the make-up of every chord you learn; some of the most common ones are given in the Appendices.

3- The third installment is to build on know-how and automatisms acquired earlier, in order to derive scales and modes by calling upon their intervallic construction (e.g. know that Phrygian is 1-♭2--♭3--4--5-♭6--♭7--8). Needless to say that your knowledge of the guitar fingerboard and note locations must be impeccable, as the least you need is to instantly spot the root/fundamental of what you are about to play. Some common scales and modes found in jazz are given in the Appendices.

As you make your way through these steps, strive for being conscious at all times of the harmonic degree of the note within the scale, arpeggio, chord or what have you, that you are playing, and as a figure of speech, you should find yourself having to make less and less of a "conscious effort" to this end. In all likelihood, you will simultaneously associate a visual mapping of those intervals on the fretboard. Note names may not be what instantaneously comes to your mind as you navigate the fingerboard, the harmonic degree or interval however, should. For example, if you are playing in A melodic minor and you are about to sound a F♯ note, F♯ may not be what comes to your mind first but the 6th of the scale should. If you are cognisant of both, you are much envied...

Soon enough, through repetition, some of these steps will be bypassed (e.g. you will know that the note two strings up from the 5th string on the same fret is a ♭7th away – no need to add intervals from 5th to 4th string and 4th to 3rd string anymore).

5- "Lessons learnt!"

Oftentimes, guitar players are restrained by chord shapes they have learnt; they would know the root, therefore they can move/transpose the chord voicing on the fingerboard (commonly with the root in the bass), but they are less aware of the function of the remaining notes which in turn translates into an inability to alter the chord, add to it, work out inversions etc.

Similarly, patterns can become roadblocks in the execution of scales. When asked to play a given mode starting on a string other than the low E string, or not on the fundamental of the mode, many guitarists first need to determine its parent scale (e.g. G major is the parent scale to A Dorian), recall the parent scale patterns they have learnt and struggle to find where in this pattern the mode fits. Heaven forbid if one were to play in-between patterns and associated fingerings; it would almost equate to learning a whole new pattern.

Another more extreme approach is to work out the notes within the chord or the mode to play (e.g. G7 is G-B-D-F), which is synonymous with finding the key signature and proceeding from there...a tedious and time-consuming operation.

If arpeggios are to be played, the guitarist might view them as a hybrid of chords and scales and resort once again to shapes or boxed positions, making the task no easier nor any faster. Meanwhile, the chord progression has moved to other places!

"Thinking intervals", you should be able to forego most of these mechanisms[13] and reach directly for the note to play and intelligently pick your notes based on their harmonic function.

Those milestones need to be cleared or at least well within sight, before you move onwards and upwards. Ensure you are headed in the right direction – it takes time to rewire old habits...

The remainder: connecting positions (from one anchor to another), changing modes within a position, building lines around chords, sequencing and playing intervals diatonically, taking advantage of fretboard symmetry, chord manipulation etc. will come with time, practise, and sound fundamentals.

The "intervallic fluency test"

A true and failsafe test to assess your progress in becoming familiar with intervals across the fingerboard is the following:

1 Pick a scale or mode of your choice, for example A major or A Lydian.
2 Set your metronome to a slow meter, such as 60 bpm.
3 Start playing one note of the chosen scale per beat, <u>across strings and all over the neck</u> (forget positions, shapes, and patterns...of course). Those notes can be played in a random fashion, or in a more systematic or even musical manner.
   To reduce the difficulty, you can start playing in one position only and later expand to the entire neck.

---

[13] Knowing patterns and shapes or even licks in general won't hurt, and can always serve the purpose of something to fall back on. However, knowing their interval construction will give meaning to otherwise "lifeless" visual representations.

5- "Lessons learnt!"

- If you succeed in playing only notes within the chosen scale without interruption <u>WHILE</u> knowing what scale degree each note corresponds to (e.g. #4th, 3rd, 7th), you are on the right track! You can move to the next step.
- If you made mistakes or paused to think what the next note of the scale should be, the tempo is too quick for you at this time and you are not ready to move on. Keep practising with your metronome set to the very same meter (or slower).

4   You can then slowly increase the tempo of the metronome and repeat the exercise.

Note that this exercise can be adapted to play groups of notes or chords on each beat. This time, you should be able to name each chord tone degree within the chord.

This test will be an honest barometer of your facility with intervallic thinking on the guitar. However arduous or even impossible it may seem at first, you will eventually become more at ease with it.

6 Chord-melody étude

Chapter 4 showed a simple example of how chords can be built around a melody or how, from a chord, melody notes can be added around it, all being enabled by a thorough knowledge of the harmonic function of each note. Generally speaking, any chord progression can be embellished by adding some melody notes around the chords. In this chapter, a more elaborate application of intertwined chords and melody is written as a stand-alone piece, falling in the broad style of *chord-melody* playing. The term *chord-solo* may also be found in the literature as a reference to this style of playing, where a single guitar takes on both the role of soloist and accompanist[14].

Chord-Melody Étude

---

[14] This is how most of the repertoire is written for solo classical guitar. In popular music genres such as rock, the melody and the harmony are often arranged as two distinct parts. In jazz, country, folk music or bluegrass, it is not uncommon to stumble on this type of playing (e.g. works by Joe Pass, Chet Atkins, Jerry Reed, Pierre Bensusan, Tommy Emmanuel).

Intervallic Fretboard – Towards improvising on the Guitar

6- Chord-melody étude

Chord-Melody Étude (1/2)

Intervallic Fretboard – Towards improvising on the Guitar

6- Chord-melody étude

Chord-Melody Étude (2/2)

In this short Chord-Melody Étude, a single (sometimes a couple) note is played after the chord, bringing out the underlying melody line that is carried throughout the piece by the single notes and the chords. Additionally, some stepwise voice leading is present within the chord changes.

Pay close attention to the harmonic function of the notes being played (underscored by the "IVL" notation), and also that those single melody notes are played around/in proximity to the chord form. Play the piece with the chords only, and then as it is written (chords + single notes). Listen to how those single notes add character and movement to the piece, elevating the chord progression to a fully-fledged stand-alone song.

7 Intervallick Rock

This chapter's focus is on intervallic thinking in a soloing context, using ideas mostly developed throughout Chapters 2 and 4. The piece strings together a series of blues and rock licks with a suggested chord progression as a backdrop.

The analysis will concentrate on the melody line which can nicely stand alone in its own right.

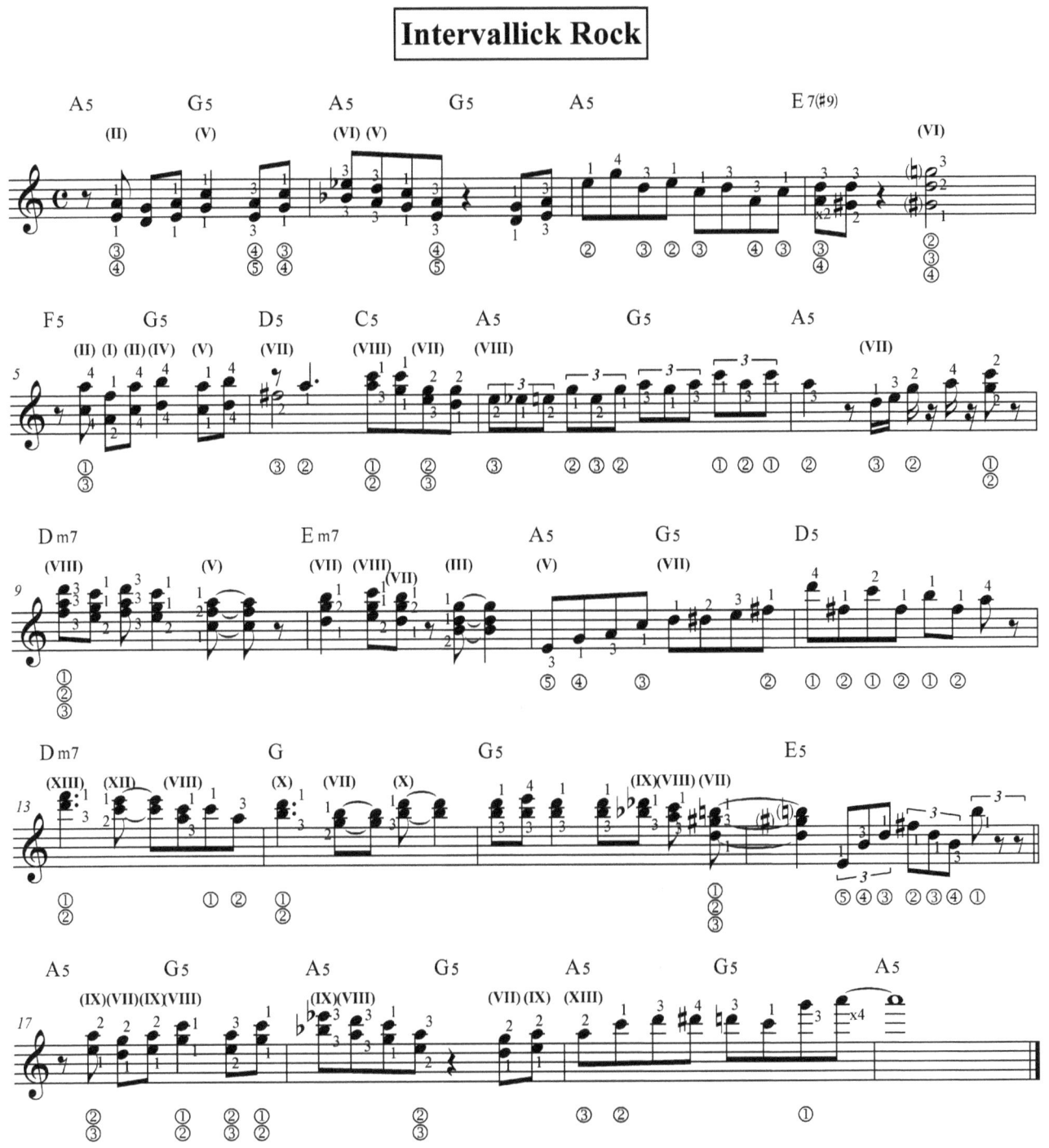

Intervallic Fretboard – Towards improvising on the Guitar

7- Intervallick Rock

Chord progression

The progression is as stripped down as it gets, so as not to overpower the melody. The melody having a stand-by-itself character, the chords are harmonically discreet – almost like a bass line. They are power chords (5 chords leaving the 3rd out), triads and the odd 4-note chord here and there (7th).

Most chords leaving out the 3rd, the progression is not as revealing as to the tonality without a little inspecting. The progression is a riff where the surrounding changes denote the key of A minor (Amin chord is never played though). Chords are taken off the A minor scale, mostly.

A natural minor (relative minor of C major) harmonised in 7th's is:
A-7 B-7(b5) Cmaj7 D-7 E-7 Fmaj7 G7

Going by the scale degrees of A minor, the progression can be likened to:
Bars 1 to 4: I-VII; I-VII; I; V
Bars 5 to 8: VI-VII; IV-III; I-VII; I
Bars 9 to 12: IV; V; I-VII; IV
Bars 13 to 16: IV; VII; VII; V
Bars 17 to 20 (return to initial theme): I-VII; I-VII; I-VII; I

Even a minimalistic harmony can be stirred up to carry a tune. A rhythmic pattern for the accompaniment is suggested above the standard music staff to lay down the groove and give momentum to the tune.

Rhythmic anticipation is a technique used in certain bars. The chord is played on the weak beat (upbeat) immediately before the next beat or measure it is actually expected in (e.g. bar 1 or bar 7). A similar idea is used in Chapter 8 for the melody. The lead sheet shows chords without rhythmic anticipation, only the detailed 3-staff system sheet displays this rhythmic device. Introduce some syncopation and 1/16th notes and you will be off to a funkier place!

Nonetheless, let's not get carried away: the rhythm is not the ambition of this exercise. Moving on to the melody...

Melody line

The melody combines licks based on intervals and scales – short ideas developed over one to two bars – and is summarised by the "IVL" staff. The explanation follows.

<u>Bars 1 & 2:</u> This is a typical blues lick in A with double-stops harmonised in 4th's.

<u>Bar 3:</u> A short sequencing bar, back-pedalling on a descending A pentatonic minor lick.

7- Intervallick Rock

<u>Bar 4:</u> Double-stops in 4th's resolve to a tritone, which contains the 3rd and ♭7th guide tones of the E7♯9 chord. The reference tone is chosen as E, not A, as the line is thought of against the chord rather than the key.

<u>Bars 5 & 6:</u> Double-stops in diatonic 6th's over F and G, followed by double-stops in 3rd's over D and C. The F♯ on D5 implies Dmaj for a moment (F♯ is not diatonic to A minor). Although chords off A minor are played, we are thinking individual chords, hence the reference tone reflecting the root of the chords.

<u>Bars 7 & 8:</u> Back to a single-note line ascending the A blues scale in triplets.

<u>Bars 9 & 10:</u> This is a series of triads with inversions over D-7 (Dmin, Cmaj, Fmaj), diatonic to D Dorian (4th mode of A natural minor), followed by the same over E-7 (Gmaj, Cmaj).

<u>Bars 11 & 12:</u> Returning to single-note playing, bar 11 is the ascending blues scale in A with an anticipation guide tone (F♯, 3rd of Dmaj) heading into bar 12. Bar 12 descends D Mixolydian with a lower F♯ pedal.

<u>Bars 13–16:</u> Diatonic 3rd's melodically over D-7 and Gmaj, with a descending chromatic pattern on beats 3 and 4 of bar 15 resolving down to the Emaj chord tones. Setting up the final section, an E7 arpeggio makes for the transition.

<u>Bars 17–20:</u> This is merely the original theme of bars 1 and 2, at the octave. To finish it off, bar 19 is an ascending blues lick in A ending on the high note A.

Intervallick Rock (1/3)

Intervallick Rock (2/3)

Intervallick Rock (3/3)

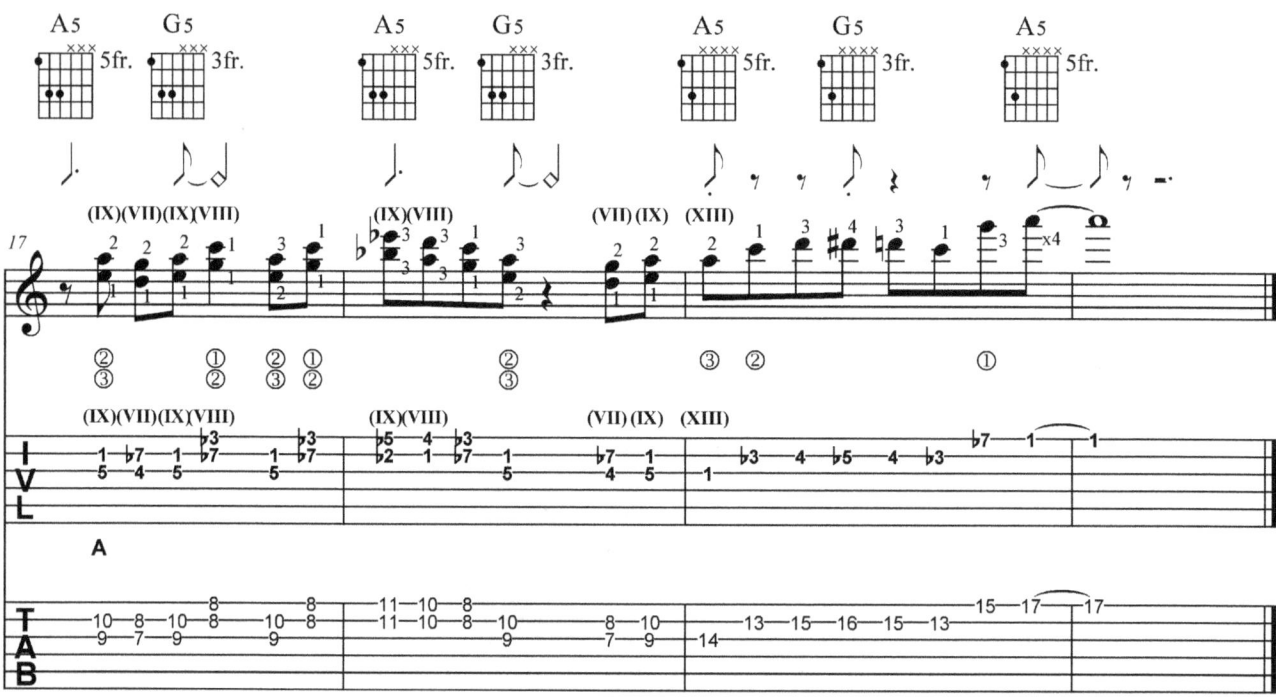

Intervallick Rock is a straightforward example of applying an intervallic approach to draw lines mostly from A pentatonic and blues scales. You are encouraged to use this progression to develop similar bite-size licks in A or take it further (e.g. play chord tones, use A natural minor scale).

8 "Rhythm Ology"

This section will bring the interval approach full circle and apply it to tackle the initial challenge posed by the jazz standard Anthropology. A solo is provided over a similar chord progression and focuses on developing lines on each chord of the progression thinking "intervals". Every bar is meticulously explained: "why am I playing these notes?" and "what am I thinking in order to play these notes?". Though jazz theory is called upon to develop the lines, this exercise aims at highlighting how an intervallic approach to soloing over changes brings out implied scales, chord tones and colour notes with little effort.

Why this song?

Anthropology is one song among many based on a chord progression or form commonly referred to as "Rhythm Changes". The terminology was coined after the song "I Got Rhythm" by George Gershwin, first published in 1930, which exhibited those changes. That song soon became a popular basis for countless heads written in the bebop era by jazz musicians. It spawned songs such as "Oleo" by Sonny Rollins, "The Theme" by Miles Davis, "Rhythm-A-Ning" by Thelonious Monk, and "Anthropology" by Charlie Parker, to name but a few. The chord progression's popularity almost rivaled that of the blues.

Tunes based on rhythm changes display a number of jazz compositional idioms in their chord progression. For that matter, we have used such a progression against which we built a solo/chorus, and appropriately named it "Rhythm Ology"! Progressions found in jazz offer a sandbox that prompts a variety of improvisational devices while paradoxically adding more boundaries than a less intricate progression (e.g. rock song). The interplay between the harmonic progression and the melody in jazz is where the difficulty resides. Hence, this sandbox proves adequate to apply an intervallic approach in the context of diverse melodic ideas.

A basic rhythm changes type progression is shown hereafter. Let us take a peek and understand some of its subtleties.

Brief song analysis

The form:
A glance at the chord changes reveals that the song breaks down into four 8-bar sections. The first two are pretty similar despite slight variations in the ending; the third section, also called the bridge, adopts a more stagnant chord progression. Finally, the last section is a return to the second section. The song's form is therefore AABA, very common in jazz. In a song such as Anthrolopology, the head or original melody pretty much follows this format too. "Rhythm Ology" however is through-composed: there is no repetition or recurrent theme in the melody.

8- "Rhythm Ology"

The key signature[15] is that of B♭ major, which is indeed the key for most of the song, as emphasised by the opening and ending chord B♭6 and the ending note of the melody, B♭. The meter (time signature) is 4/4. The tempo and style are Bebop, which is usually greater than 200 bpm (but we don't have to play it that fast!), and implies a swing feel rather than the notated straight eighth notes.

The changes:

The song's changes, also known as rhythm changes, are by no means trivial. Bar 1 confirms the key signature with an entire measure of B♭6, before moving to a classic II-V in bar 2, followed by B♭6 (I chord) in bar 3. The next chord in bar 3 is G-7 which is the VI and is a diatonic substitution for I, i.e. bar 3 is a variation of bar 1. Bar 4 is the same as bar 2 (II-V). Bar 5 is another II-V (in the key of E♭ however), going from F-7 to B♭7, which kicks off a series of dominant 7th chords moving in a cycle of 4ths (B♭7, E♭7 and A♭7) – these chords are dominants of one another. The first ending, made of bars 7 and 8, sports a standard III-VI-II-V (or a set of two II-Vs). Note that in jazz lingo, the VI is loosely referred to in this combination, as it is not a minor but a dominant chord (G7). An alternate explanation, yet less common, of the first ending is to consider D-7 (III) as a diatonic substitution for I, followed by a secondary dominant G7 (V/II) anticipating the II-V turnaround in bar 8.

The second time around, the A section is just the same, while the final bar marks the key centre with a full bar of B♭6 – a cadential point.

Note that bars 5 and 6 could have been explained with borrowed chords from the parallel key B♭ minor but that would be more fitting in classical rather than jazz harmony.

The bridge, or B section, is a series of dominant chords moving through the cycle of 4ths, while never quite establishing the key by only offering a lingering dominant chord over two bars (as such, calling it modulation to other keys would be a little exaggerated). This allows a great deal of freedom in the melody. The final two bars are over F7, which is the V of the song's key of B♭ major, and prepares nicely a return to the initial form in the last section.

The last section is merely a repetition of the first section with the second ending. As an idiosyncrasy (due to habit), we wrote it with E♭-7 instead of E♭7 in the 6th bar of the last A' section (30th bar). That transforms the bar into another II-V.

The melody:

The melody or head sometimes adds tonal information where the chord changes may leave a question mark. In our case, we have written a melody to these rhythm changes in "Rhythm Ology", the analysis of which follows in the next section.

---

[15] B♭ major harmonisation in 7ths: B♭Δ C-7 D-7 E♭Δ F7 G-7 A-7(♭5)
B♭ natural minor harmonisation in 7ths (parallel key): B♭-7 C-7(♭5) D♭Δ E♭-7 F-7 G♭Δ A♭7

Basic "Rhythm" Changes

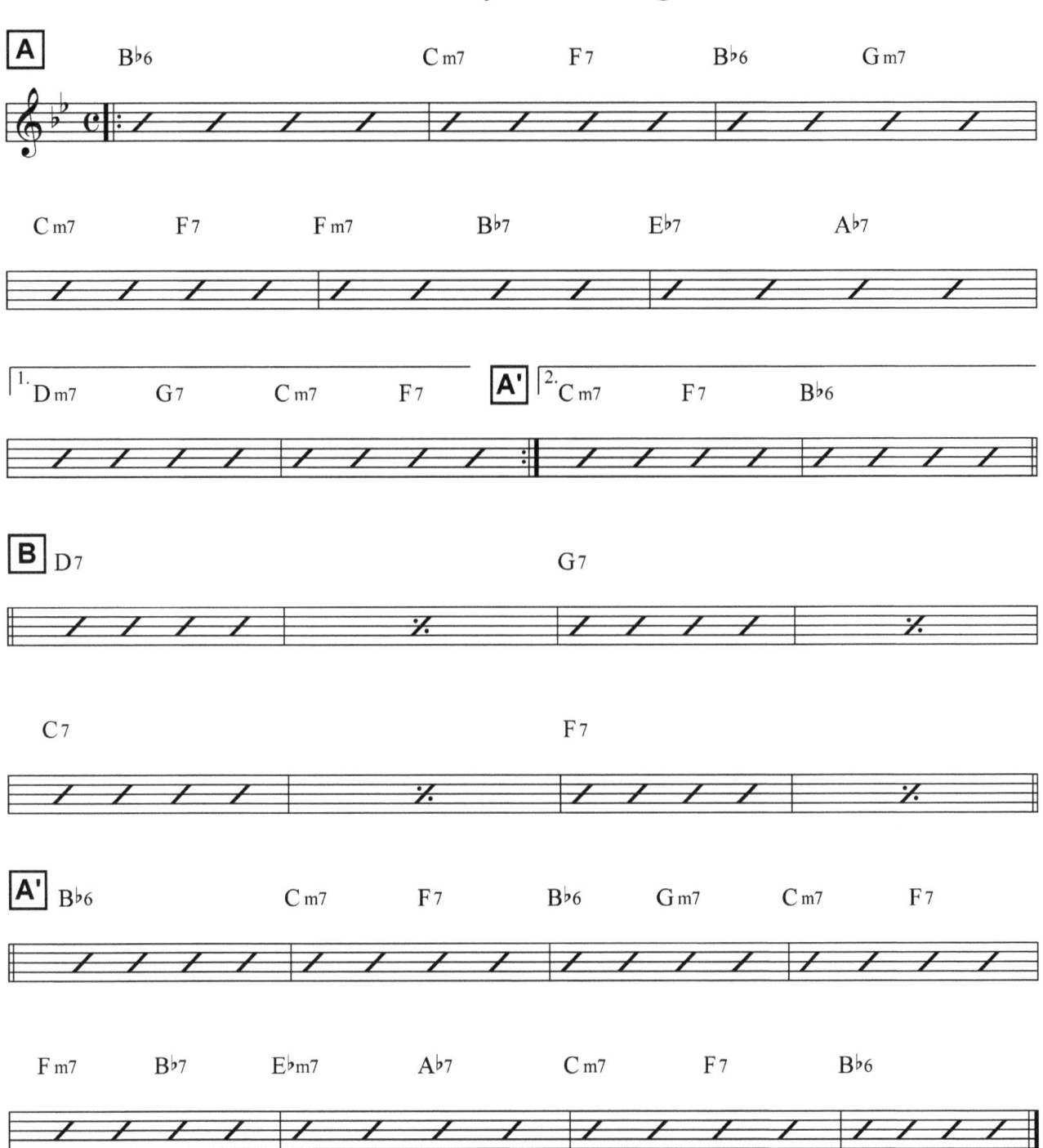

8- "Rhythm Ology"

Piecing it all together: applying jazz improvisation techniques through an intervallic thought process – commented solo

As a wink to the improvisation assignment that opened this book, we are now going to apply some of the intervallic concepts we covered in the context of a "real life" chorus improvised over the basic rhythm changes. The term "improvised solo" is in fact a euphemism. It isn't exactly improvised, as it is not spontaneous but carefully thought out. Because it was meant to showcase principles covered in this book, it is structured accordingly. Nevertheless, it remains an improvised solo, only a calculated one!

Improvisation techniques frequently found in jazz are used, deliberately resorting to a given technique every two bars or so. Unlike typical jazz standard heads, there is no recurring theme; rhythmic complexity was avoided in order not to distract from the notes themselves, and so was ornamentation.

Notation-wise, the interval-based notation system of Appendix B is the "pièce de résistance", laying bare the harmonic function of each note, thereby putting the intent of the improviser and the techniques used in the spotlight. Standard music notation supplements it with rhythmic information, while tablature is added for the sake of completeness (a word of advice is not to rely on tablature here).

Of note is the fact that the entire solo is played in 5th position, occasionally utilising position extensions (x1 and x4). This is a testament to the versatility of the guitar neck but even more that a thorough understanding of the fretboard map can open astounding possibilities. There is a lot one can do in one position, and erratic shifts and jumps from one position to another during a song – a symptom pertaining to playing patterns and shapes – are often unnecessary.

All at once, "Rhythm Ology" may appear as a leap in the dark, although the previous chapters have shed a great deal of light on what's at hand. Study the piece a couple of bars at a time, as you feel comfortable. You should strive to almost "sight-read" the interval-based notation system. You will see throughout the analysis of the solo that scale degrees, chord tones, and connecting changes via guide tones are the essence of what drives the improviser, and the interval-based notation spells out those very characteristics.

8- "Rhythm Ology"

8- "Rhythm Ology"

Let us walk through the solo:

Section A:

Bars 1 & 2: Guide tones (3rd, 7th of chords) are emphasised with half step resolution, as they are an important aspect of hearing the chord changes. The first note A is the 7th of B♭6 (so to speak) and the first bar ends on D, which is the 3rd of B♭6. This transitions nicely by half a step into E♭ which is a guide tone of C-7 (♭3rd). Ascending diatonically, the chord change from C-7 to F7 is punctuated by another half step guide tone to guide tone transition (B♭, ♭7th of C-7 to A, 3rd of F7), while the last note E♭ (♭7th of F7) resolves once again by half a step into bar 3 (D, 3rd of B♭6). Guide tones truly underscore the chord changes despite playing off the B♭ major scale for the entire two bars – in fact, guide tones paired with their skillful placement in the melody will let you hear the chords pass by (without even playing the chords).

Bars 3 & 4: Chord tones make up these two bars, with a little rhythmic variety (syncopation).

Bars 5 & 6: The idea of chromatic passing tones is developed here. Notes are grouped in 4-note cells, and the passing tones mingle with chord tones which help ground the chords on strong beats. The second note E makes for a chromatic run over F-7. B♭7 is also covered in half steps, ending on A which creates a tension point on a weak beat, as it is not part of B♭7. Bar 6 pursues the same idea, developing a close-knit chromatic line over E♭7 and ending once more on a tension point B (not in E♭7, nor in the following A♭7 chord). However, B does pave the way for a smooth transition into the next chord A♭7 by landing on C (3rd of A♭) by half a step.

Bars 7 & 8: Over this III-VI-II-V harmony, some rest is offered to the listener as evidenced by the slowdown in the rhythm. This signals the end of section A and sets up for section A'. In bar 7, a line based on guide tones is played, but in intervals of 4ths and tritones, which is a sharp contrast to the previous bars, more chromatic. This sparseness in tonal distance also echoes the sparseness in the rhythm, and truly accentuates an overall impression of roominess.

Another technique at play is anticipation, which here consists in playing into the next chord before it is actually sounded: the end of bar 7 alludes to C-7 by playing its guide tones E♭ and B♭, and in bar 8, the A half note (3rd of F7) is a strong cliché to F7, two whole beats before the actual chord. The reference note C in the "IVL" notation was accordingly placed a whole beat before the C-7 chord, and so was the note F, two whole beats before the F7 chord.

8- *"Rhythm Ology"*

Solo/Chorus to "Rhythm Ology" (1/4)

Intervallic Fretboard – Towards improvising on the Guitar

Section A':

Bars 9 & 10: Bar 9 opens this new section with a bang, picking up the pace with an ascending diatonic sequence in B♭ major over B♭6 with rhythmic similarity (pattern of triplets). Bar 10 is using a 4-note arpeggiated cell over C-7 and its retrograde inversion over F7. It steps into the next bar with a tie on the 3rd of B♭6 (D).

Bars 11 & 12: The idea at play in these two bars is essentially to draw notes from the B♭ major scale while approaching certain notes by a non-diatonic neighbouring tone (bar 11: D♭ to D and E to F; bar 12: E to F). The reference note in "IVL" notation is written as the root of the chord, because the thread of thought was the chord and intentional placement of guide tones. Nevertheless, since the lines are very scalar in B♭ major, B♭ would also be a reference note candidate in its own right (particularly in bar 12).

Bars 13 & 14: These two bars form a unit of ascending followed by descending arpeggios of the chords in the progression.

Bars 15 & 16: C-7 is arpeggiated and so is F7. The last bar of section A' is another cadential point where a rest and a half note bring section A' to an end. Observe that the last note, F (5th of B♭6), is the 3rd of the next chord D7 – a guide tone.

8- "Rhythm Ology"

Solo/Chorus to "Rhythm Ology" (2/4)

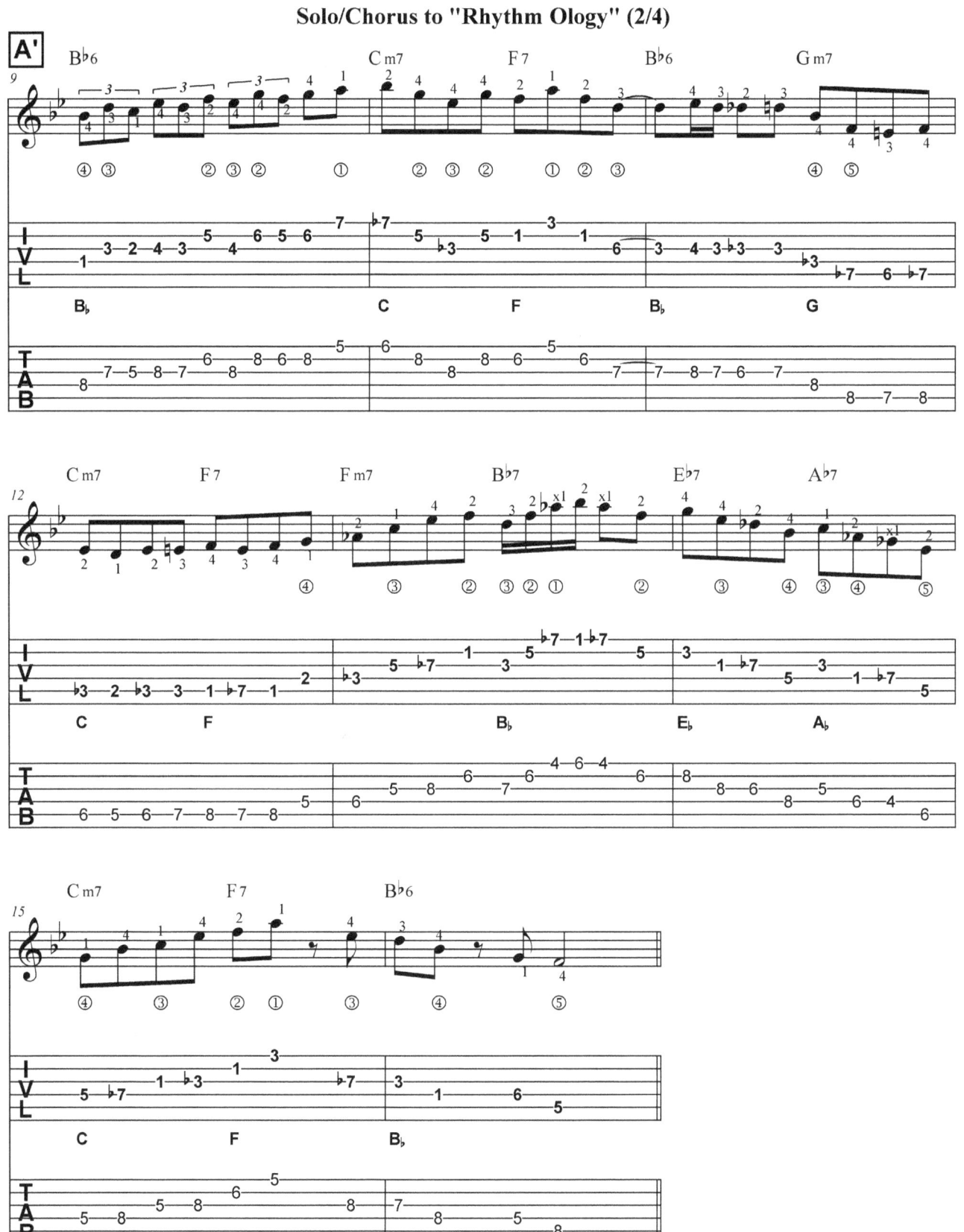

Intervallic Fretboard – Towards improvising on the Guitar

Section B:
As stated in the paragraph on the form, the bridge "leaves" the key of the song, temporarily, and so does the melody! Although taking on the appearance of four 2-bar measures of dominant chords, the melody really transforms the bridge into a superstructure comprised of two 4-bar phrases.

<u>Bars 17 & 18:</u> Bar 17 is based on arpeggios of D7 and D13, with some lower neighbouring tones creating the impression of sporadically weaving in and out of the chord. Bar 18 is much the same, though a little more scalar in D Mixolydian. The ♭3rd to 3rd passing tone in the triplet adds a bluesy element. The last note E sets up a half step connection into the ♭7th (guide tone) of G7.

<u>Bars 19 & 20:</u> Bar 19 develops a 4-note cell idea made of descending 3rds of G Mixolydian. Bar 20 remains in G Mixolydian, starting on a guide tone (3rd), and gives a slight break to the listener, halfway through the bridge (end of first half of the superstructure). The next half, the superstructure rhythmically resumes through an ascending triplet with a diatonic pick-up note A.

<u>Bars 21 & 22:</u> Bar 21 uses heavy chromatic runs. Bar 22 starts on the ♭7 of C7 and descends stepwise (except for a passing tone) and beat 3 starts on F (4th of C Mixolydian) which is a suspension resolving to E (3rd) on beat 4.

<u>Bars 23 & 24:</u> After moving through the cycle of 4ths, the last two bars of the bridge fall back on F7, the dominant chord of the song's key of B♭ major (which will resolve into the tonic B♭6 chord in the next section). Bar 23 is reminiscent of the 4-note descending cell in 3rds that played out four measures earlier over G7 (bar 19); this time, it is in F Mixolydian, except for the last note A♭ which does not belong to the scale. The ultimate bar leaves the listener with an intriguing ear twister, almost a question mark with scarce notes, outside the ongoing harmony (C♯), creating a sense of expectancy.

8- *"Rhythm Ology"*

Solo/Chorus to "Rhythm Ology" (3/4)

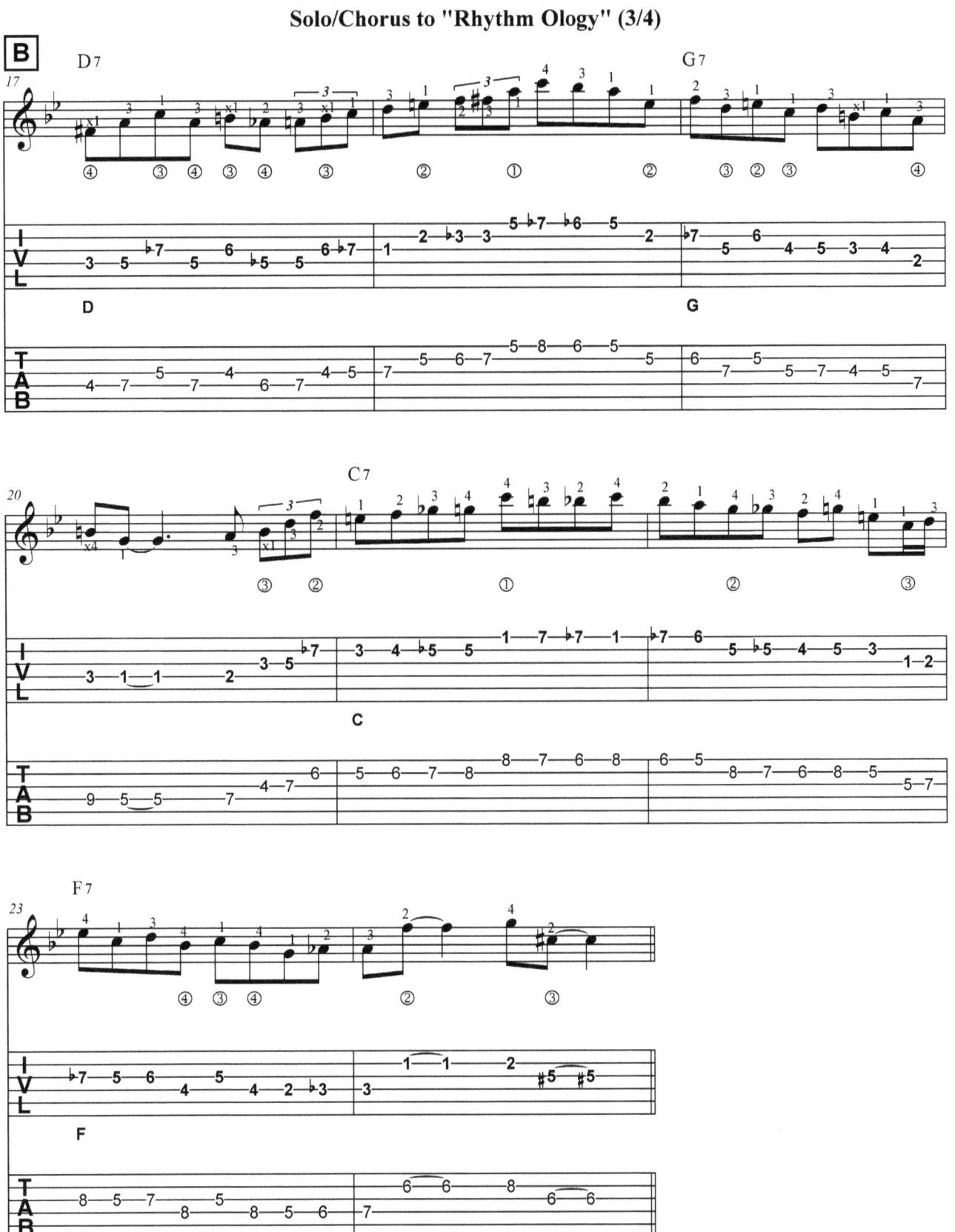

Intervallic Fretboard – Towards improvising on the Guitar

8- "Rhythm Ology"

Section A' (last):
This last section is a return to the initial progression making up the first and second sections.

<u>Bars 25 & 26:</u> Bar 25 is a return to the melody of section A with a slight variation. A rhythmic change embodied by a diatonic triplet in B♭ signals this new section, which continues diatonically throughout the measure, but for a lower neighbour note on beat 2, and ends on the 3rd on the upbeat of beat 4, preparing for a half step resolution into E♭ (♭3rd of C-7) on the downbeat in bar 26. Bar 26 starts with a typical bebop figure of ascending stepwise motion, leaving C-7 on the ♭7 (B♭), resolving down half a step against F7 to A (3rd of F7). The line then jumps up a major 6th enharmonically (it really is a diminished 7th as written) to G♭, which is the ♭9th of F7. This altered tone adds interesting dissonance and is a common bebop cliché. The bar concludes on E♭ (♭7th).

<u>Bars 27 & 28:</u> Once again, the previous bar moves smoothly into bar 27 by half a step, from one guide tone to another (♭7th of F7 to 3rd of B♭6), which is a technique used many times over in this solo in particular and jazz in general. Beats 3 and 4 form a descending G-7 arpeggio. Bar 28 is a diatonic run that is almost the B♭ scale verbatim, starting on G, with the exception of skipping A. Notice the careful placement of guide tones against F7 (starts on ♭7, ends on 3rd). Again, B♭ could have been chosen as the reference note in the "IVL" notation for this bar.

<u>Bars 29 & 30:</u> Bar 29 is actually linked to the preceding bar, as it is practically a copy of that bar played backwards (retrograde). Guide tones emphasise each chord change on the first and last notes, resolving by a whole step to G♭ (♭3rd of E♭-7) in bar 30. The line carries on downwards in bar 30, marking A♭7 by its 3rd, C.

<u>Bars 31 & 32:</u> Bar 31 is a copy of bar 28 against the same C-7 to F7 progression, except for the last beat which begins on the ♭9th of F7, in a triplet cell, transitioning to the final measure by a half step guide tone to guide tone connection. The last bar is simply a jump by a minor 6th to B♭, the root/fundamental of the chord/key, which sounds very final.

"Rhythm Ology" is no small feat: a lot of material to digest. Take parts of the progression and make the melody your own. For example, in the first two bars, following some of the intervallic principles described in Chapter 4 and improvisation techniques exposed in the melody, develop a line over B♭6 in the first bar. You could choose to stay in the 2nd position, play B♭6 chord tones, add extensions (9th, 11th etc.), or play a scalar line based on B♭ major or any of the three pentatonic majors contained in B♭ major (B♭, E♭, F pentatonic major). As you make your way to bar 2, practise leaning into it with a guide tone of C-7, either in the same position or connecting to another position on the fretboard. This song can be used as a springboard to experiment and test your understanding of intervallic thinking and soloing techniques.

8- "Rhythm Ology"

Solo/Chorus to "Rhythm Ology" (4/4)

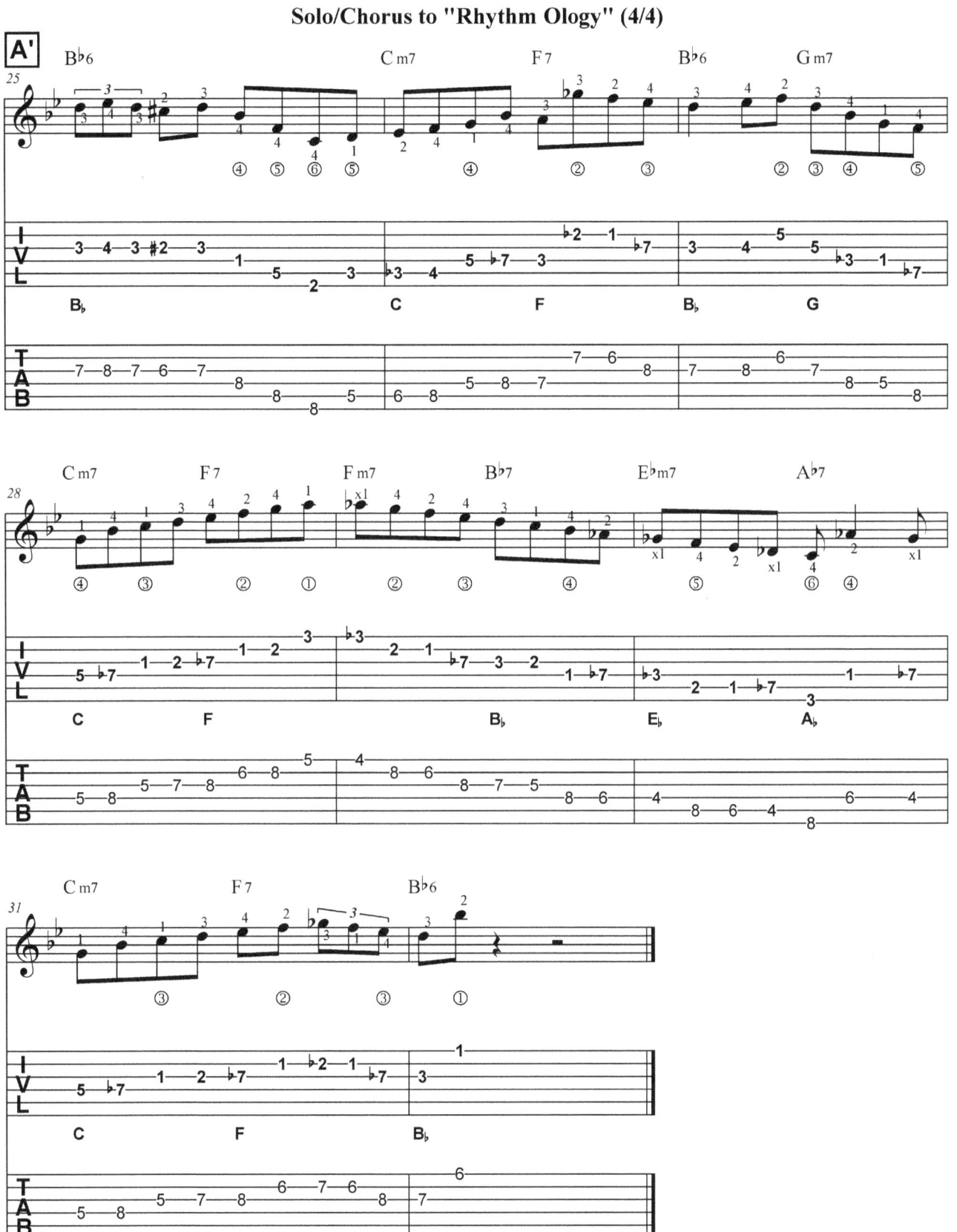

Intervallic Fretboard – Towards improvising on the Guitar

Chord comping over "Rhythm Ology"

Equally as important as the melody is the harmony to "Rhythm Ology". Pursuing our intervallic approach, we will now look into elaborating on the basic chord progression found on the lead sheet, while applying several principles addressed in earlier chapters (e.g. chord tone degrees, non-root intervals, chords without the root, chord homonyms).
An analysis, measure by measure, follows. Compare this richer harmony, more likely to be played in a jazz context, to the basic rhythm changes.

Section A:
Bar 1: The tune begins with a B♭6, which is just a variation on the major chord, adding the 6th. B♭maj9 is next: the root and the 5th of the previous chord voicing are retained while the 6th moves up a step to the 7th and the 3rd moves down a step to the 9th.

Bar 2: A common II-V makes up this bar: a standard C-7 moving to an altered dominant F7♭9. The E♭ (♭3rd of II and ♭7th of V) is the common tone between the two chords.

Bar 3: F7♭9 resolves to B♭6 (I chord) as expected before moving down to G-7 (VI chord) of the key, a common variation of I (diatonic substitution).

Bar 4: Another II-V here, this time using natural extensions: C-7 is played as C-11 while the F7 is played as F13. Root position dominant 7^{th}s are seldom used in jazz.

Bars 5 & 6: Next is a "stock" minor 7th voicing of F-7 with stepwise movement from the previous F13 (3rd to ♭3rd and 13th/6th to 5th). This is another II-V going to B♭9 and keeping the common tone C, 9th of B♭9 – it may appear as though the common tone C undergoes a large intervallic jump, but it doesn't at all, the same note is played on the 3rd string 5th fret in B♭9 instead of the 2nd string 1st fret in F-7.
The B♭9 is the first in a series of three dominant chords moving in a cycle of 4^{th}s to E♭9 and A♭13. These chords are dominants of each other (B♭9 is V of E♭9 which is V of A♭13, but we move in the opposite direction in 4^{th}s instead of 5^{th}s). The chords could also be altered, if desired (i.e. ♭9, #9, #11/♭5, or ♭13/#5), but are played with natural extensions.

Bars 7 & 8: The first ending of section A is a standard III-VI-II-V (or two sets of II-Vs). It starts off with a D-11 going to a heavily altered G7#5#9 which is the V of C-7. The A# (#9) of G7#5#9 becomes the ♭7th of C-7 and the D# (#5) becomes the ♭3rd of C-7...a judicious voice leading.
The C-7 then voice leads very smoothly to F13(9), keeping the common tone G on the top of the chords (5th of C-7 = 9th of F13(9)).

Section A':
Section A' up to the second ending can use the same comping as in section A.

Bars 15 & 16: We start with a C-7/B♭ and a smooth half step descending bass line leads to the F9/A

change (from ♭7th of C-7/B♭ to 3rd of F9/A).
We then move up half a step (with the bass) to B♭ for B♭maj7, amidst which the bass note shifts from the 6th to 5th string – there is no large interval jump, only a change in strings. B♭add9/D is an inversion change to add diversity. Remember that this last bar is no other than a variation over an entire bar of B♭ major chord (B♭6 – see lead sheet).

Section B:
Bars 17 & 18: The bridge – a series of dom7th chords in 4ths – starts with a D13 with the F# (3rd) on top. The F# moves up half a step to G to become the 11th in the D11 change.
The G continues moving up by half a step to become the #11th in D7#11 before ascending a minor 3rd to end as the 13th in D13. Instead of an otherwise "dull" D7 for two full measures, we managed to create some interesting harmony based on the dominant sound through voice leading the top note on the 2nd string. The other chord tones are maintained relatively motionless. Intervallic awareness is an enabler in voice leading.

Bars 19 & 20: Same exercise over G dominant. We voice lead from the D13 to a G9 (observe how all chord tones move minimally only by half or a whole step, except for the root D, moving up a 4th to G). The next chord breaks up the voicing with a G/F or G7 (3rd inversion of G7) and then G9/B (2nd inversion of dom9th). Last, we voice lead the F (♭7th) down to E (13th) for G13.

Bars 21 & 22: More of the same over C dominant. C13 strikes and voice leads the 13th down a step while retaining the other pitches for a C9. Notice the absence of root for these chords. Can you picture homonyms? (E-7♭5...)
The 9th of C9 is then raised to #9 for C7#9 before lowering it down again a whole step to D♭ for C7♭9 (two altered dominant chords). The ♭9 is further lowered by a half step to C, the 5th of F7.

Bars 23 & 24: The final section of the bridge starts off with a root position dominant 7th, which is rare, but is immediately moved up diatonically to G-7, and then by half a step to A♭°7 as a passing chord, before ending on a F7#5. This last altered dominant chord has an A on the bottom to allow for the bass line to move by a half step only to B♭maj (the bass line in these two bars went F-G-A♭-A) and the progression in the last section A' starts over.

Section A' (last):
The last section (A') can use the same chord changes as the second section (except for the E♭9).

An intervallic understanding of chords and their make-up, beyond moveable shapes, is enlightening and food for thought, indeed! The individual chord tones as well as the connection from one chord to the next are put forth.
Once again, work through the analysis a couple of bars at a time – do not rush, fully digest the construction of each chord and chord tone movements.

8- "Rhythm Ology"

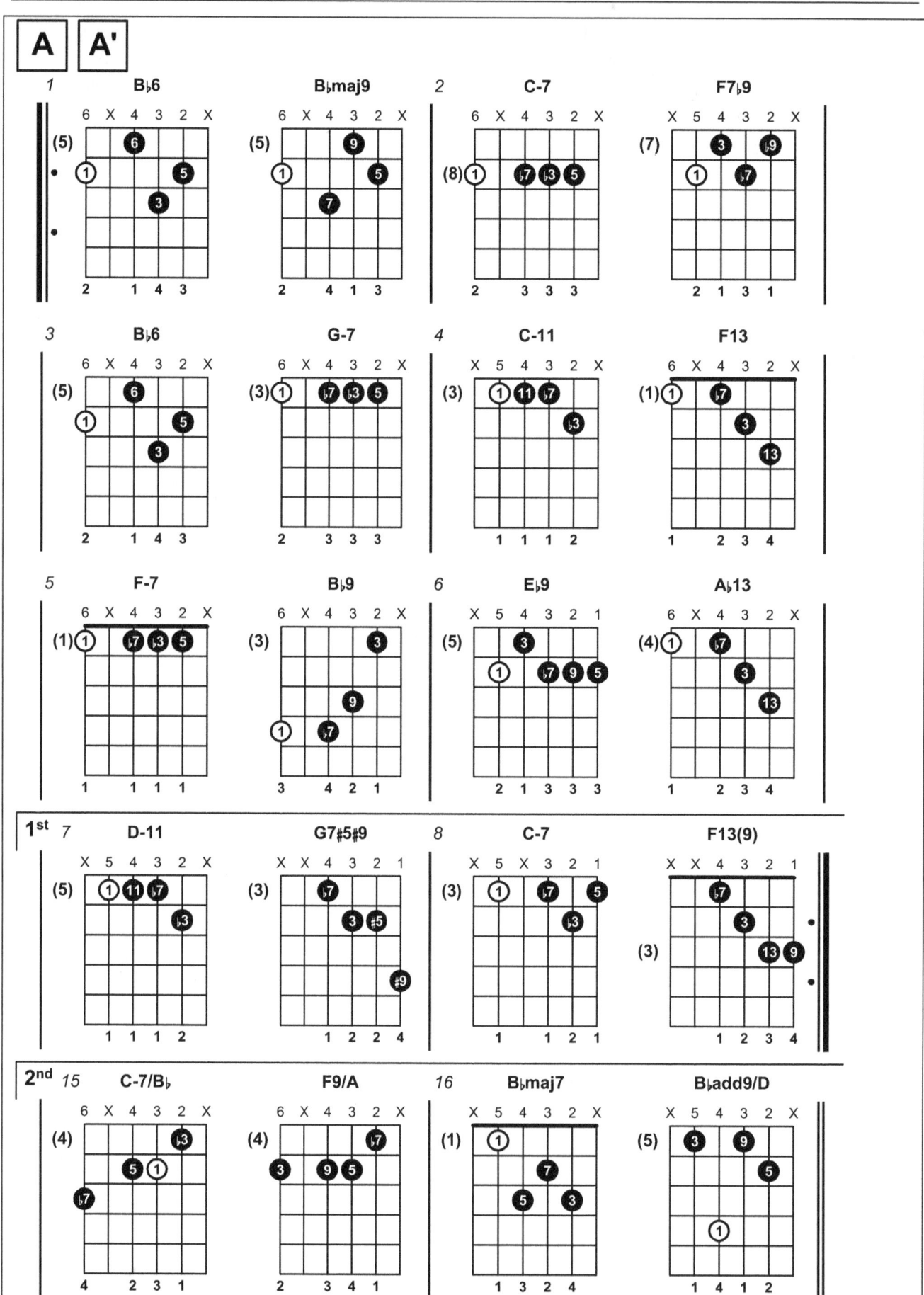

8- "Rhythm Ology"

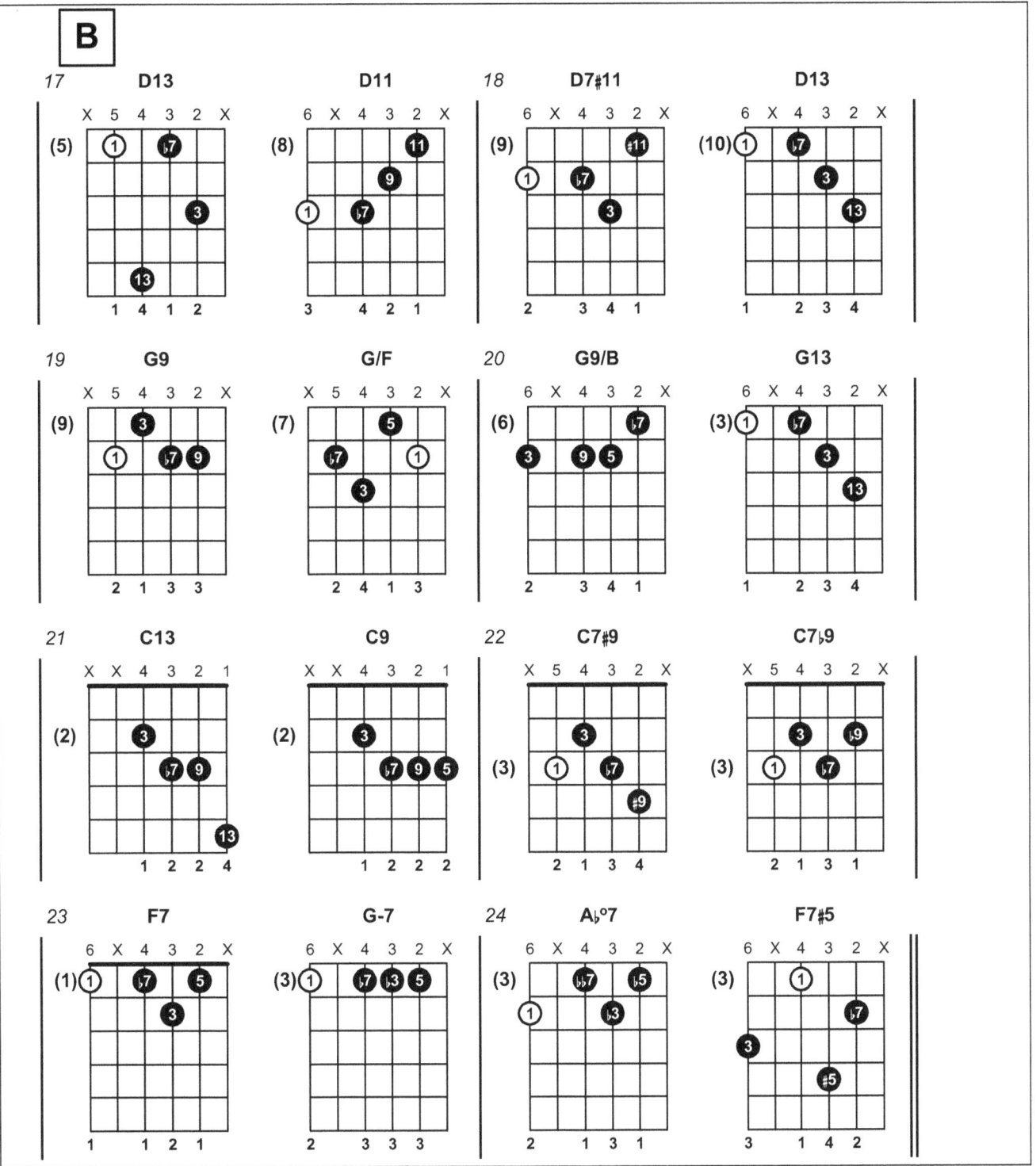

APPENDICES

Appendix A

Interval jogger

Recognise these intervals as fast as you can, from the lower to the higher pitch and vice versa. You can make up similar exercises of your own.

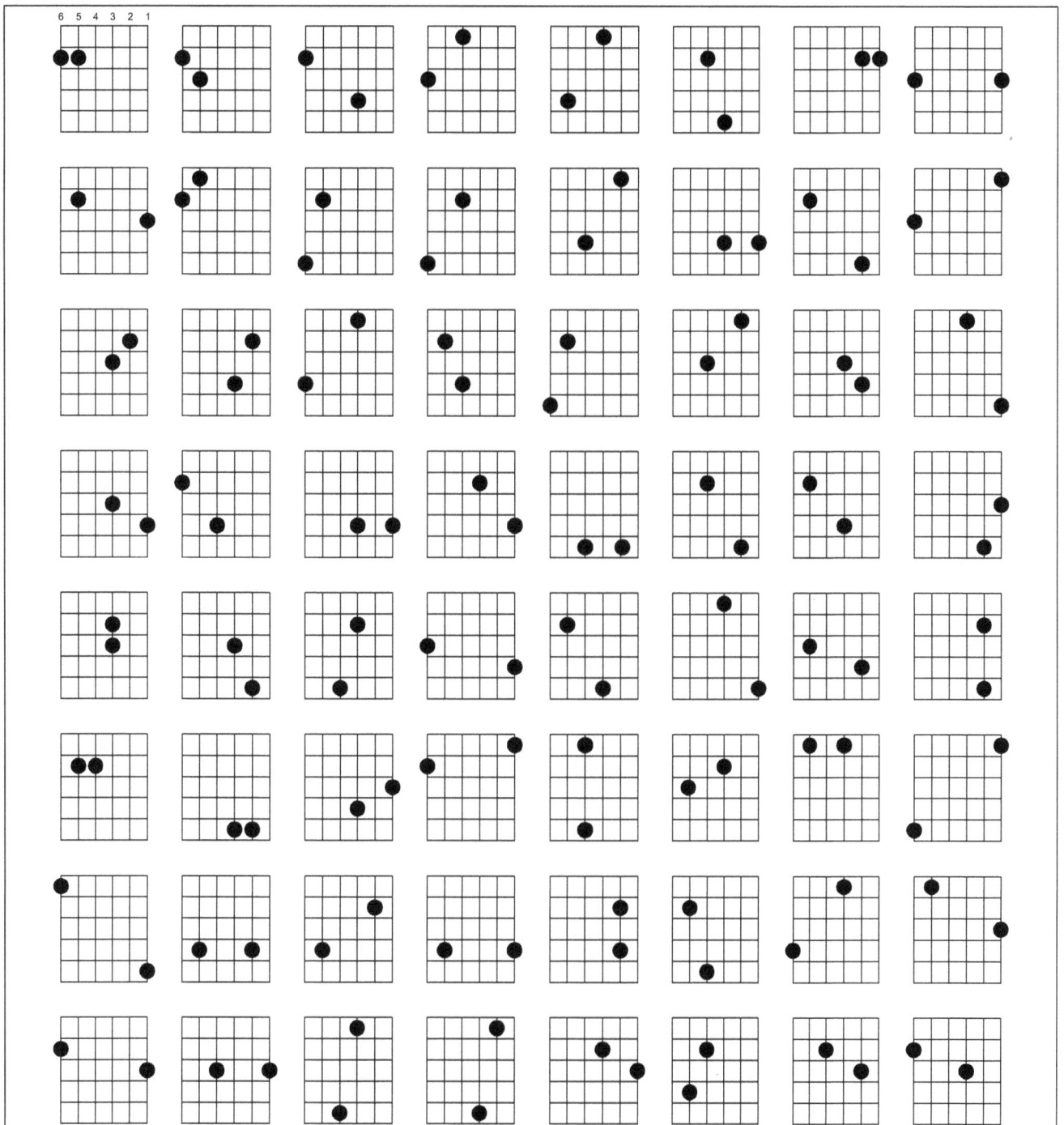

Appendix B

Interval-based notation system

As the focus in this book is on intervals, we have devised a notation system that, like standard music notation and tablature, will enable music transcription while highlighting intervals. This unfamiliar notation staff labelled "IVL" is paraded throughout the book, accompanying standard notation and tablature.

Although we deliberately let it sneak in at the very beginning of this text, it is only properly laid out here, separately, as we felt a good command of string intervals (Chapter 2) is a prerequisite to grasp the relevance and applicability of this notation. After completion of this section, you may want to return to the exercises in previous chapters, concentrating on this system. This symbolic notation device should stimulate your training in "thinking" and "seeing" intervals.

This notation system makes use of position playing, which is well known to guitarists. A recap is given here.

Position playing

Position playing is commonly used on the guitar and we provide here a brief reminder, as it will be put into use further on. Figure 58 will serve as the thread for the description.

Figure 58 shows position playing in 4th position, corresponding to the entire neck from frets 4 to 7. The numbered black circles refer to the frets the corresponding fingers would typically play. The position of the finger #1 (index) gives the number of the position (4 here), finger #2 (middle) would then fret the next fret up, across all strings, finger #3 (ring) the following fret and finger #4 (pinkie) would fret the 7th fret. In general, the thumb behind the neck stays put while playing in a given position.

B- Interval-based notation system

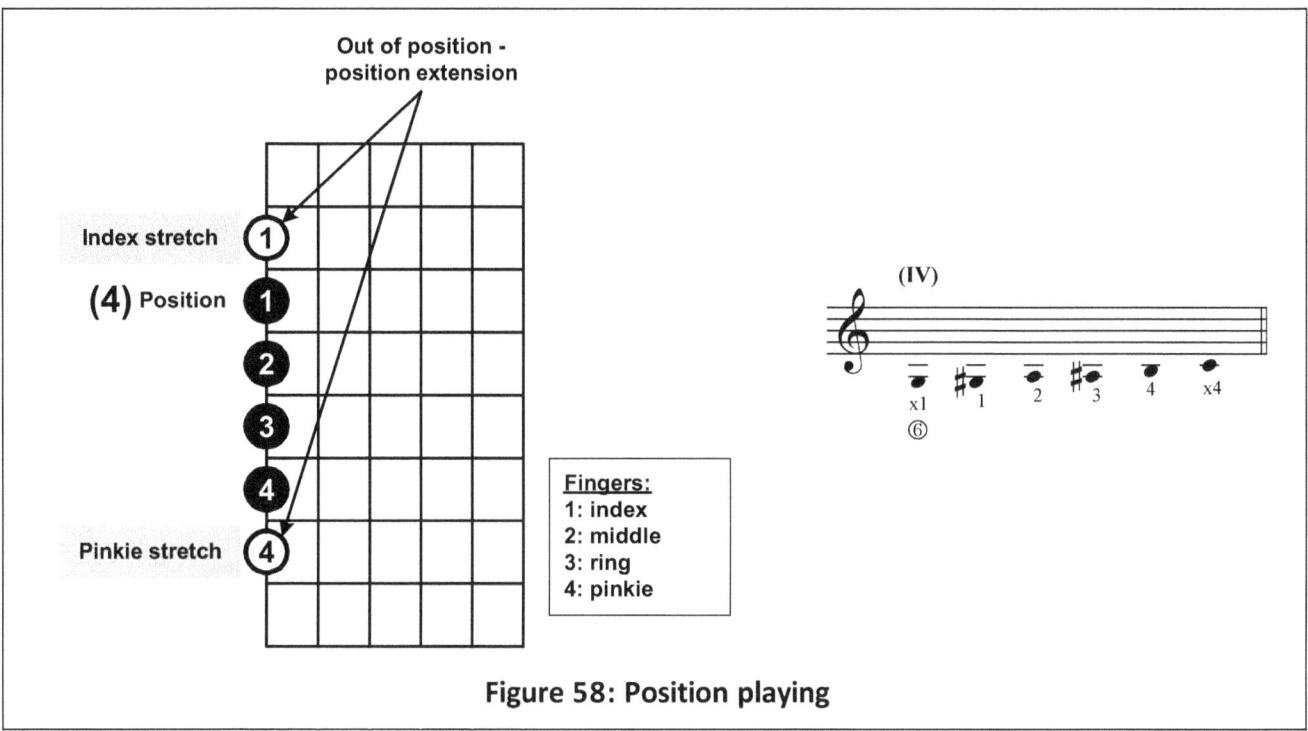

Figure 58: Position playing

An interesting corollary to position playing comes from the white circles, numbered 1 and 4, corresponding respectively to the index and the pinkie. As indicated, those frets would still fall under the 4th position, but require an extension of the index for the former and an extension of the pinkie for the latter, thereby extending the coverage of one position to 6 frets. By extension, we infer that the fretting hand's thumb behind the neck does not move positions as we stretch our index or pinkie. Furthermore, the 2nd and 3rd fingers (middle and ring) will stay put and always play the one fret assigned to each of them. Extensions of the index and pinkie are marked x1 and x4 on the music staff. On occasion, you may come across extensions of the middle and ring fingers, noted x2 and x3 (e.g. in blues).
Across all 6 strings, the coverage is 36 frets, without requiring a position change. It amounts to two octaves and a perfect fourth. That's quite a range!
For chordal fingering, position playing cannot be easily applied...common sense takes over. Fingerings for chords in this book are just that: an indication of what finger frets which note.

Another approach to increase the coverage on one string is *expanded position playing* or *expanded fingering*, often used in three-note per string scale/motifs (sometimes even four-note per string). We will not cover this type here. Fingering is a rather personal preference and guitarists may adopt one or the other or combinations (or other types) depending on the situation – just be aware that several options are available to you and that one size does not fit all! Hence, the fingerings listed in this manuscript, based on position playing, are merely guidelines.

A good exercise consists of running chromatic drills in a given position, with the stretches (extensions noted x1 and x4), up and down the strings. Example 22 in the 5th position is given in groups of four $1/8^{th}$ notes, although playing five notes on most strings (watch for the accents). Beware of those wide stretch intervals as you are playing (minor 2nd). Along with a metronome, this

B- Interval-based notation system

ordinary exercise can turn into an extraordinary springboard for practising fretting/picking hand synchronisation, finger independence (change finger sequence and include alternating strings), picking technique (alternate, economy, legato), string skipping, rhythm changes (e.g. change to triplets), accents (e.g. accents on second half of beat 1, grouping of 5 instead of 4 notes) etc. However, don't take the easy route and play this example mechanically, keep relative intervals in mind so that you know where you are. Otherwise, it will take the form of yet another pattern and you will get lost on the fingerboard: don't allow your fingers in the driver's seat, let your mind guide your fingers!

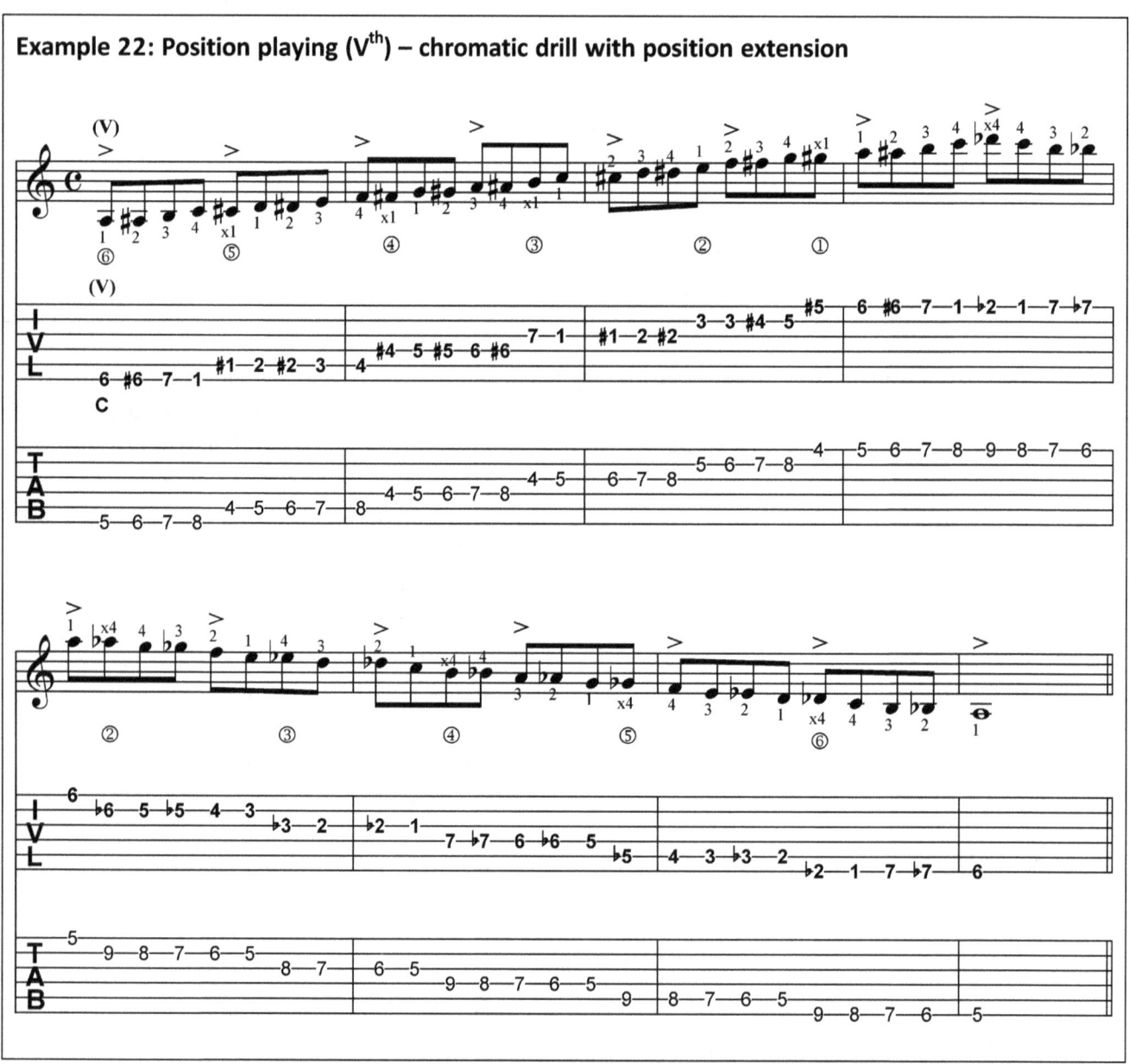

Example 22: Position playing (Vth) – chromatic drill with position extension

B- Interval-based notation system

Description of the system

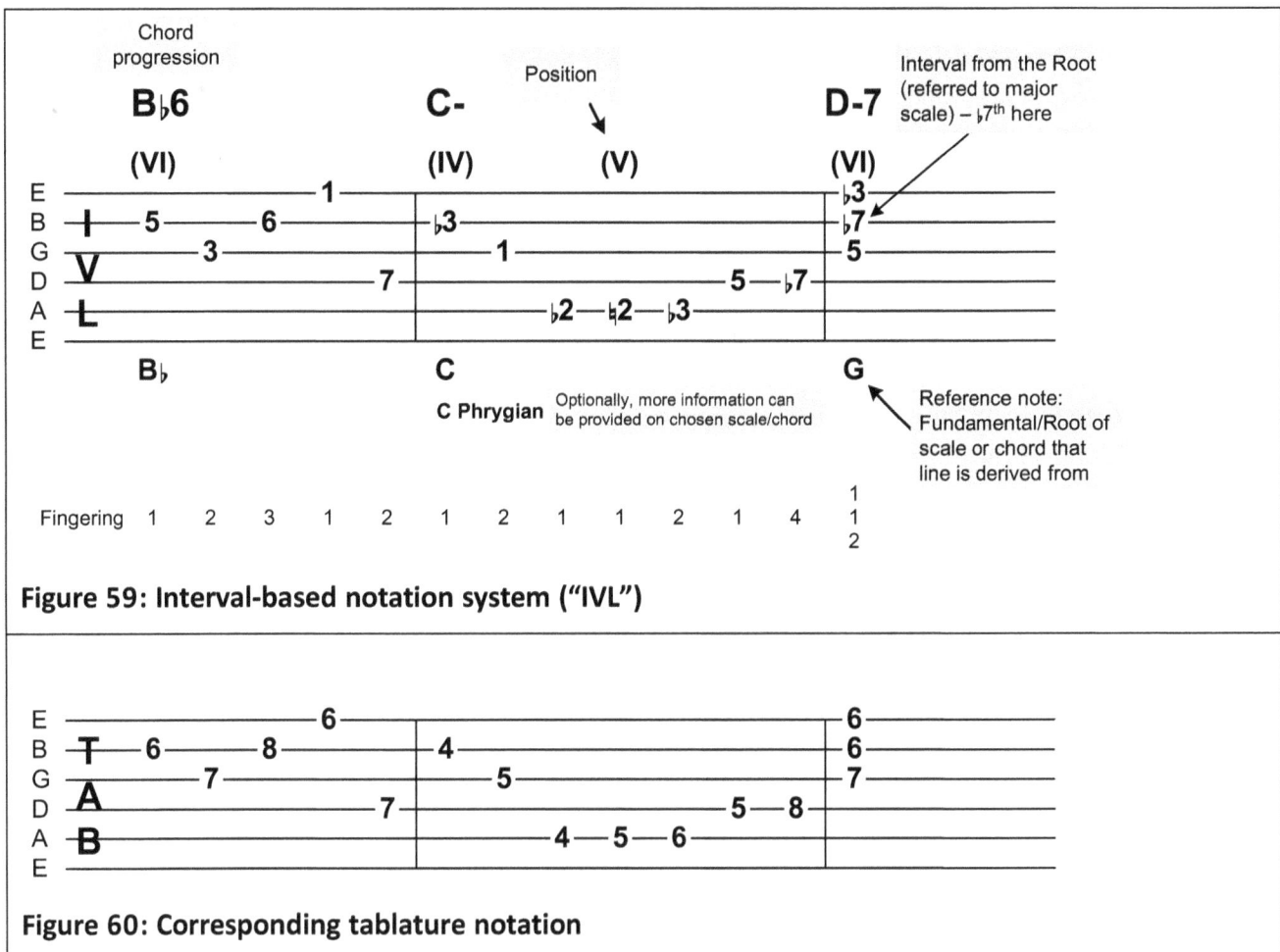

Figure 59: Interval-based notation system ("IVL")

Figure 60: Corresponding tablature notation

The notation system that is introduced in this section aims to solidify an intervallic thought process and visualisation thereof on the fingerboard. It requires familiarity with the material covered in Chapter 2. If anything, this notation can be an appropriate educational tool.

The system employs the six strings of the guitar as its canvas – the notation staff – like tablature notation. However, the numbers that populate each string are intervals, referred back to a fundamental or root (or tonal centre), given below the staff[16]. Finally, position playing is used by indicating above the staff a suggested position where to play those intervals. Fingering is left at the discretion of the player but the position will generally dictate the fingering.

At this point, having your guitar in hand might ease comprehension. Looking at Figure 59, the first bar is over a B♭6 chord. The intervals are referred back to B♭, as noted below the staff. It is a hint

---

[16] For simplicity, one could argue that instead of placing the reference tone below the staff, it could take the place of "1" on the staff itself, and that would lighten the notation a little. Unfortunately, the reference tone or "1" may not be played in a given bar (or only played by another instrument such as a bass), therefore we opted to keep the reference tone indication detached from the staff.

that notes will be coming off the B♭ major scale (or its modes). The first note on the staff is the 5th on the B string – that is the note F (5th of B♭ major) – it is left for you to find that near the 6th position, that note is located on the 6th fret. Similarly, the next note on the staff is the 3rd on the G string – that is the note D (3rd of B♭ major) – which you will recognise in the vicinity of the 6th position as being located on the 7th fret. And so on...

Look at Figure 60 to confirm your understanding of the note location from the tablature notation.

Moving on to the second bar, the chord is now C- and the reference note is C. Therefore, intervals will be referenced back to the C major scale. However, the presence of ♭2 and ♭3 implies the C Phrygian mode (♮2 is a passing note). Note that midway through the bar, a position change to the 5th position occurs, although still referring intervals back to C.

The last bar is over a D-7 chord. We are in 6th position, and interestingly, the reference note is not D, but G. Furthermore, the vertical alignment on the staff naturally is the sign of a chord being played. 5, ♭7, and ♭3 make for a G-7 chord, omitting the root! (also known as a B♭ major triad)

The reference note (or reference tone) is a key indicator of the player/composer's intention. For example, if a passage is in the key of C major but the line derives from E Phrygian, using E as the reference note is the most meaningful choice. Or, if still in C major, but the line is now based on a G7 arpeggio, using G as the reference note will highlight the arpeggiated chord tones. If however, everything was referred back to C, the E Phrygian and G7 arpeggio will be diluted in the notation and harder to see. Another example is in the context of anticipation: if the current chord is A7 and one starts to play a line into the next chord D-7 (while still against A7), then adopting D as the reference note would account much better for what is being played than A. The choice of the reference note is therefore arbitrary, but some choices are much wiser than others.

Rhythmic information can either be directly written on the staff, as sometimes is the case with tablature, or better, on the regular standard music notation staff.

To avoid complexity and confusion, only simple intervals are penned down on the staff: compound intervals are written as their corresponding simple intervals (i.e. you will not encounter 9th, 11th and so forth on the staff but 2nd, 4th etc.).

In retrospect, this notation, not unlike standard music notation, leaves some degree of freedom for note location. It does not specify/dictate the particular string/fret combination to fret a given note. The notation by itself does not readily convey dependencies between bars[17] but picturing the intervals on the fingerboard will add to that dimension. The primary information this system carries is the function of the note (i.e. interval), as opposed to the standard staff's primary information which is the note's name and tablature's primary message, which is the location of the note on the fingerboard. By "primary", we infer what generally comes to mind first. In a sense, it is reminiscent of figured bass notation in classical music.

---

[17] An interesting extension to this notation would be to introduce signage to delineate those dependencies (e.g. anticipation of a guide tone of the next chord), at the expense of burdening the staff.

B- Interval-based notation system

For clarity, there is no key signature in this notation. Accidentals are notated at every occurrence, even if in the same measure. The implied key signature is that of the tone centre, pointed out below the "IVL" staff.

Position playing indication can be marked strictly (it has been in the example given), or instead, rather freely. Like standard music notation, approximate position will be sufficient, making the staff less burdensome (e.g. in the example provided in Figure 59, the position change in the second measure could have been left out for the player to figure out).

It is a powerful system that will foster intervallic thinking appending immediate meaning to the note being played (functional harmony). For example, if the chord in the progression is Cmaj9(#11), playing the #11 (or #4) will appear clearly on the notation.

As a summary:
- Standard notation: conveys primarily <u>note name</u>
- Tablature: conveys primarily <u>note location</u>
- This notation system (interval-based): conveys primarily <u>note harmonic function</u>

To gain from this notation system and ultimately from intervallic thinking, one must focus their attention on this notation system, and only use tablature as an additional help to confirm note location, and traditional music notation for rhythm. It visually synthesises the intervallic approach and its merits.

That being said, the authors strongly encourage any serious guitarist to be proficient at reading standard music notation. It will not only enhance your comprehension of music but also facilitate communication with other musicians, open up a vast repertoire of music to you etc. Tablature is convenient and requires less of a learning curve, but its limitations will later surface time and time again.

Appendix C

Common and less common scales & modes

A variety of scales and their modes are described here, based on their intervallic make-up. The applications of those scales are beyond the scope of this book and can be found in many other theory or jazz publications.

Nomenclature:
- The hyphen character "-" is used to symbolically represent a half step in the construction of the scales. For instance, a whole step is notated by two hyphens "--", thereby also giving a visual representation of the distance between two consecutive notes in the scale.
- Roman numerals are not used as it is customary, to represent scale degrees. Instead, regular "Arabic" or Western numerals are used.
- As is common practise, all scales and modes are referred back to the major scale in terms of interval quality as well as numbering (even when they have fewer than 7 notes like the pentatonic scales).
- Although the major scale only contains 7 notes, an eighth note is added at the end of the scale, which is merely the same note as the fundamental (and could be noted "1" instead of "8"), simply to underline the interval between the last note of the scale and the fundamental at the octave.
- The characteristic note(s) is what distinguishes a scale or mode from the major or the minor scale.

Scale (or mode)	Construction	Typical chord	Relationship (and characteristic notes)
Ionian	1--2--3-4--5--6--7-8	maj7	major
Dorian	1--2-♭3--4--5--6-♭7--8	-7	(minor with ♮6)
Phrygian	1-♭2--♭3--4--5-♭6--♭7--8	sus♭9	(minor with ♭2)
Lydian	1--2--3--♯4-5--6--7-8	maj7(♯11)	(major with ♯4)
Mixolydian	1--2--3-4--5--6-♭7--8	7	(major with ♭7)
Aeolian	1--2-♭3--4--5-♭6--♭7--8	-♭6	natural minor
Locrian	1-♭2--♭3--4-♭5--♭6--♭7--8	ø	(minor with ♭2, ♭5)
Pentatonic major	1--2--3---5--6---8	7	(major minus 4 and 7)
Pentatonic minor	1---♭3-4--5---♭7-8	7	(minor minus 2 and 6)
Blues	1---♭3--4-♭5-5---♭7--8	7 or -7	(pentatonic minor + ♭5, or pentatonic major + ♭3)
Diminished	1--2-♭3--4-♭5--♭6-♮6--7-8	o7	(1 step, 1/2 step etc.)
Whole tone	1--2--3--♯4--♯5--♯6--8	+	(1 step, 1 step etc.)
Melodic minor	1--2-♭3--4--5--6--7-8	minmaj7	(major with only ♭3; or minor with ♮6, ♮7)
Harmonic minor	1--2-♭3--4--5-♭6---7-8	minmaj7	(major with only ♭3, ♭6; or minor with ♮7)
Modes of melodic & harmonic minor			see References
Altered dominant (7th mode of melodic minor)	1-♭2--♯2-3--♭5--♯5--♭7-8	altered dom7	(contains all alterations to a dominant 7th chord)

Intervallic Fretboard – Towards improvising on the Guitar

Appendix D

Common chord formulae & symbols

Variations in notation and definition can be found in the literature. For example, a dom11 chord sometimes includes the 9th, and often leaves out the 3rd (due to dissonance between the 3rd and 11th which really makes it a sus chord).

Chord Name	Common Symbol	Formula
Major	none (just note name)	1–3–5
Major (6th)	6	1–3–5–6
Major 7th	maj7, Δ or Δ7	1–3–5–7
Major 9th	maj9, Δ9	1–3–5–7–9
Major 11th	maj11, Δ11	1–3–5–7–11 (rare: tension)
Major 13th	maj13, Δ13	1–3–5–7–13
Major add 9th	/9, add 9, (9)	1–3–5–9 (no 7th)
Major 6/9	6/9	1–3–5–6–9 (no 7th)
Minor	min, -	1–♭3–5
Minor (6th)	-6	1–♭3–5–6
Minor 7th	min7, -7	1–♭3–5–♭7
Minor 9th	min9, -9	1–♭3–5–♭7–9
Minor 11th	min11, -11	1–♭3–5–♭7–11
Minor 13th	min13, -13	1–♭3–5–♭7–13
Minor add 9th	min/9, min add 9, min(9)	1–♭3–5–9 (no 7th)
Minor 6/9	-6/9	1–♭3–5–6–9 (no 7th)
Minor major 7th	minmaj7, -Δ7	1–♭3–5–7
Dominant 7th	7	1–3–5–♭7
Dominant 9th	9	1–3–5–♭7–9
Dominant 11th	11	1–3–5–♭7–11
Dominant 13th	13	1–3–5–♭7–(9)–13
Altered dominant	7(♭9); 7(#9); 7(♭5); 7(#5)	1–3–5–♭7–♭9 etc.
Suspended	sus, sus4	1–4–5
2	2	1–2–5
Add 9th suspended	/9 sus	1–4–5–9
Augmented	+	1–3–#5
Diminished	o7	1–♭3–♭5–♭♭7
Half-diminished	ø, min7(♭5), -7(♭5)	1–♭3–♭5–♭7
Slash chord (triad over bass note, i.e. inversion of triad, or over other note)	/ (e.g. D♭/A♭) (e.g. D♭/C = D♭maj7)	D♭maj triad with 5th in the bass (A♭)

Intervallic Fretboard – Towards improvising on the Guitar

Notation guide

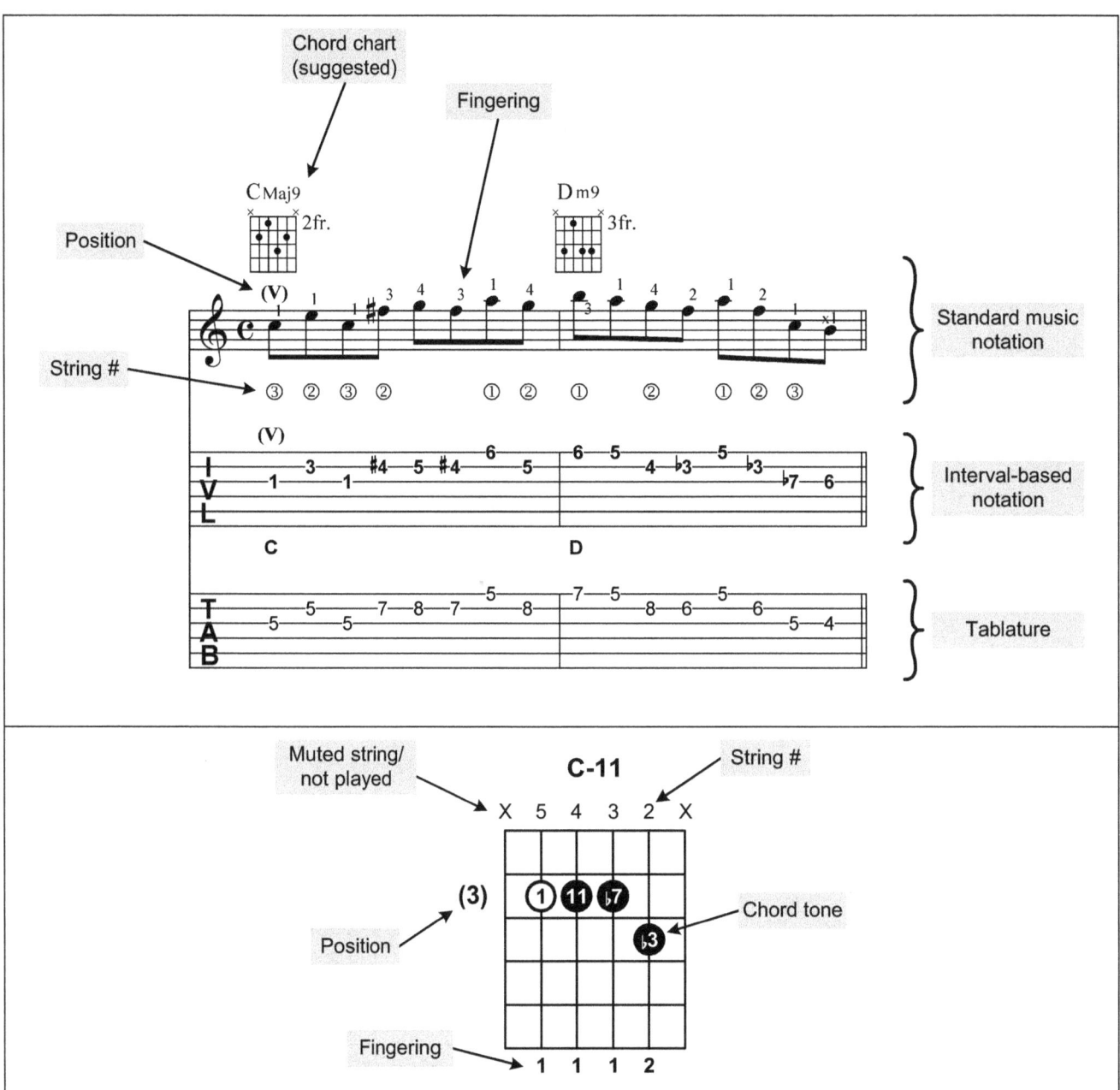

Note: The notation staff labelled "IVL" is explained in Appendix B titled "Interval-based notation system". Although your intuition may help you make sense out of this curious notation, it is recommended that you read Appendix B in conjunction with Chapter 2.

References and further reading

This is a non-exhaustive list of references the authors have used in preparing this book or that could serve as a starting point for further study.

[1] Arnie Berle, *Patterns Scales & Modes For Jazz Guitar*. New York, NY: Amsco Publications, 1994.
[2] Jimmy Bruno, *No Nonsense Jazz Guitar*. Hot Licks DVD. New York, NY: Music Sales Corporation, 2005.
[3] Jerry Coker, *Complete Method For Improvisation*. Van Nuys, CA: Alfred Publishing, 1997.
[4] Larry Coryell, *Larry Coryell's Jazz Guitar – Volumes 1–3*. DVD. Sparta, NJ: Stefan Grossman's Guitar Workshop, 2005.
[5] A. Danhauser, *Théorie De La Musique*. Paris, France: Éditions Henry Lemoine, 1994.
[6] Al Di Meola and Bob Aslanian, *A Guide to Chords, Scales, & Arpeggios*. Wayne, NJ: 21st Century Music Productions, 1985.
[7] Joe Diorio, *Fusion Guitar*. Van Nuys, CA: Alfred Publishing, 1997.
[8] Frank Gambale, *Acoustic Improvisation*. DVD. Van Nuys, CA: Alfred Publishing, 2007.
[9] Frank Gambale, *Chopbuilder*. Warner Bros. DVD. Van Nuys, CA: Alfred Publishing, 2002.
[10] Frank Gambale, *Technique Book 1–2*. Van Nuys, CA: Alfred Publishing, 1989.
[11] Brett Garsed, *Rock Guitar Improvisation*. DVD. 2004.
[12] Daniel Gilbert and Beth Marlis, *Guitar Soloing*. Milwaukee, WI: Hal Leonard, 1997.
[13] Daniel Gilbert and Beth Marlis, *Advanced Guitar Soloing*. Milwaukee, WI: Hal Leonard, 2002.
[14] Ted Greene, *Chord Chemistry*. Van Nuys, CA: Alfred Publishing, 1981.
[15] Ted Greene, *Jazz Guitar – Single Note Soloing – Vol. 1*. Van Nuys, CA: Alfred Publishing, 1981.
[16] Peter Huttlinger, *A Guitarist's Guide To Better Practicing*. DVD. Woodstock, NY: Homespun Tapes, 2003.
[17] Mark Levine, *The Jazz Theory Book*. Petaluma, CA: Sher Music Co., 1995.
[18] Ashkan Mashhour, *CHEATSHEET Music series*. www.cheatsheetmusic.com, 2010.
[19] Brent Mason, *Nashville Chops & Western Swing Guitar*. Hot Licks DVD. New York, NY: Music Sales Corporation, 2006.
[20] Steve Morse, *Power Lines*. DVD. Van Nuys, CA: Alfred Publishing, 2007.
[21] Dave H. Murdy, *Intermediate Training For The Modern Guitarist*. Murdy Music Publishing, CA, 1994.
[22] Joe Pass, *Jazz Lines*. DVD. Miami, FL: Warner Bros. Publications, 2004.
[23] John Petrucci and Askold Buk, *John Petrucci's Wild Stringdom*. Miami, FL: Warner Bros. Publications, 2000.
[24] Joe Satriani, *Guitar Secrets*. Port Chester, NY: Cherry Lane Music, 1993.
[25] Mike Steinel, *Building A Jazz Vocabulary*. Milwaukee, WI: Hal Leonard, 1995.
[26] Scott Tennant, *Pumping Nylon*. Van Nuys, CA: Alfred Publishing, 1995.
[27] George Van Eps, *Harmonic Mechanisms For Guitar Vol. 1–3*. Pacific, MO: Mel Bay Publications, 1980.
[28] Keith Wyatt and Carl Schroeder, *Harmony & Theory*. Milwaukee, WI: Hal Leonard, 1998.

The end (not bitter!)...

This book gradually built intervallic awareness on the guitar, eventually leading to a thought process allowing real-time construction of scales and chords with an acute understanding of the harmonic function of each note. This departs from traditional views mainly relying on memorising patterns and shapes.

Manipulating intervals should eventually become second nature. However, viewing a melody from an interval perspective may not immediately underline commonalities between a chord and the next chord in a harmonic progression – at least not without picturing the fingerboard – nor allow the execution of high speed improvised lines, which would typically call upon memory (or "muscle" memory), for instance. Therefore, an intervallic approach by itself is not the be-all and end-all to a boundless topic such as improvisation, but it is hopefully a "giant step" in that direction.

We hope that this book has tickled your imagination and will continue to unlock doors for you, while raising your fretboard savvy and broadening your horizons towards improvisation.

Back cover photograph and text

Synopsis for *"Intervallic Fretboard – Towards improvising on the Guitar"*, **by Ashkan Mashhour and Dave H. Murdy.**

Shapes and patterns are widely used in teaching the guitar, be it for scales, chords, or arpeggios. Although convenient at first, this strongly visual understanding of the guitar proves very limiting in bridging music(ality) and functional harmony to the instrument. This book takes a novel and radically different approach to the guitar, emphasising the importance of an intervallic thought process.

Based on the actual experiences of a student and his guitar teacher, we take you on a journey through intervals, gradually building fluency starting from string intervals all the way to scale and chord derivation via anchors. Along the way, we show some ideas of how to take advantage of this intervallic thought process and the guitar's inherent geometric properties. The premise of this book is to move away from shapes and patterns and become intimately familiar with intervals on the guitar, thereby leading to an intelligent choice of notes based on their harmonic function.

This fretboard know-how is exemplified through meaningful short exercises and fully-fledged pieces such as a chord-melody, a blues/rock tune, and a jazz composition demonstrating the versatility and the value of intervallic thinking.

www.ingramcontent.com/pod-product-compliance
Lightning Source LLC
Chambersburg PA
CBHW080521110426
42742CB00017B/3192